GREAT GARDENS
OF THE BERKSHIRES

By Virginia Small

Photographs by Rich Pomerantz

Down East

Text copyright © 2008 by Virginia Small.

Photographs © 2008 by Richard Pomerantz.

Library of Congress Cataloging-in-Publication Data
Small, Virginia, 1952-
Great gardens of the Berkshires / by Virginia Small ; photographs by Rich
Pomerantz. -- 1st ed.
   p. cm.
ISBN 978-0-89272-748-3 (hc : alk. paper)
1. Gardens--Massachusetts--Berkshire Hills. I. Title.
SB451.34.M4S63 2008
712.09744'1--dc22

                2008026429

Design by Chilton Creative

Printed in China/ OGP

5   4   3   2   1

Down East
BOOKS·MAGAZINE·ONLINE
www.downeast.com

Distributed to the trade by National Book Network

For Alice Christensen,
who inspired me to become
a gardener
~ VS ~

For my wife, Celia,
with whom I wish I could
share every garden I visit
~ RP ~

CONTENTS

Foreword, by Rick Darke 7

Introduction 8

I A RICH LEGACY OF PUBLIC GARDENS: **Culture, Cultivation, and Visionary Creators** 10

The Mount: The Revival of Edith Wharton's Gracious Gardens 13

Naumkeag: An Artful, Groundbreaking Collaboration 21

Chesterwood: The Sculptural Sensibility of Daniel Chester French 29

Ashintully: A Symphony on the Land 37

Berkshire Botanical Garden: A Multifaceted Community Gem 43

II INSPIRING PRIVATE GARDENS: **Passions, Personality, and Playing with Nature** 50

Little Sutton: Emily Rose's Garden of a Lifetime 53

A Warm Palette in the Garden: Thomas Gardner's Rustic Eden 59

Following a Vein of Ledge: Ian and Madeline Hooper's Rockland Farm 65

Balancing Vistas and Intimacy: Lee Link's Garden 73

Good Dogs Farm: Maria Nation Weaves Tales in Her Garden 81

Cultivating Simplicity: Nancy McCabe's Garden 89

Nature's Exuberance within a Grid: Jack Hyland and Larry Wente's Garden 95

A Formal Country Garden: Bunny Williams Creates Many Moods 103

Seekonk Farm: Honey Sharp's Garden Celebrates Color and Texture 109

Following Zen Principles: Ruth Adams's Serene Mountaintop Haven 115

A Plant Lover's Paradise: Diana Felber's Garden, Under the Hemlocks 123

Trailblazing Minimalism: Jon Piaseki's Gardened Woodlands 129

Acknowledgments 136

Noteworthy Gardens, Landscapes, and Museums 138

Community Resources 142

Nurseries and Garden-Related Enterprises 143

Garden Tours and Open Days 144

Suggested Reading 144

FOREWORD

Great gardens tell of relationships between people and place, and the same is true for great garden writing. Though plants and patterns are often a garden's most obvious signatures, its deepest, most durable capacity to inspire derives from its story. Virginia Small understands this implicitly, and has put her considerable warmth and artistry into telling the stories of the great gardens of the Berkshires. Richly nuanced and alive with humor and spirit, her first-hand observations articulate the resonant qualities of the area's historic and iconic landscapes as well as those of modern gardens still in the making.

Put a rock at your back and an eye to the horizon and imagine: Just what kind of garden would you make if presented with the opportunities and challenges of the Berkshire landscape? The region's strength of character is readily apparent in its rolling, forested vistas, its rugged outcrops, broad meadows, and clear waters. The thin soils and intensely seasonal climate take a while longer to know, and all of this requires a fair amount of experimentation before it can be settled into a coherent vision.

Despite being born of the same region, the gardens in this book are hardly alike. Selected for inclusion because they are true in their own ways to the Berkshires, they express a great range of approaches and are suitably distinct in their meanings and motivations. Music, literature, and sculpture inform more than a few, while others explore themes of color and seasonality, honor and memory, loss and discovery, renewal and reinvention. Many of the gardens have multiple personalities and function on a number of different scales, offering both intimacy and immensity.

Author Virginia Small's and photographer Rich Pomerantz's long relationships with the New England landscape, as residents and landscape professionals, enable them to bring a deep sense of the Berkshires to this book. Virginia's ear for story and process has been refined through a lifelong focus on the people and personalities behind creative design in the cultural landscape. Rich's eye sees both the bold drama of sculpted hedges and the subtle slant of the Berkshires' autumn sun, and his photographs are an elegant match to Virginia's words.

Great Gardens of the Berkshires amply demonstrates how varied and broadly informative a regional study can be. Taken as a whole, the North American landscape can seem almost incomprehensibly diverse. Contrary to the notion that there might be, or should be, an American garden style or story, this book revels in the uniqueness of a region—the Berkshires—and delves deeply enough to reveal how local portraits can provide universal inspiration. Both reflective and forward-looking, this book is sure to energize anyone seeking to integrate storytelling and a celebration of place in the making of gardens. ❦

Rick Darke
April 2008

The author converses with gardener Emily Rose as they enjoy a bucolic Berkshire vista.

Introduction

The Berkshires' undulating hills, ancient rockeries, spectacular vistas, and other natural features have long captured the fancy of artists, gardeners, and others inspired by beauty in the landscape. This book celebrates some of the creative zeal that has infused this region's gardens for more than a century.

Starting in the mid-1800s, Lenox, Stockbridge, and other towns in western Massachusetts that were settled by European immigrants began attracting wealthy families who wanted to "summer" in the Berkshires. Just a few hours from Manhattan or Boston by train, and later by car, the region became a popular getaway for those who cherished country pleasures. Writers, painters, and other artists began moving to the Berkshires, as did philanthropic individuals eager to foster a rich cultural atmosphere.

Writers Nathaniel Hawthorne, Herman Melville, and Edith Wharton and artists Frederic Church, Thomas Cole, and Daniel Chester French were among those who moved to the region. In 1932, modern dancers came here to experiment within the Berkshires' scenic seclusion and formed a troupe called Jacob's Pillow. The Boston Symphony Orchestra made Tanglewood in Lenox their summer home, and the Williamstown Theatre Festival developed a legendary summer series. The area continues to thrive as a cultural mecca, with countless performing and visual arts venues, museums, and rich historical traditions and museums.

Some great gardens of the Berkshires were developed in the late 1800s and early 1900s, a time known as the Gilded Age, when wealthy families began to build mansions in the country that they referred to as "cottages." Over time, many of those opulent homes fell into decline or were converted to new uses, and their gardens no longer exist. However, several estates, such as Chesterwood and Naumkeag, remain much as their creators conceived them. The gardens at The Mount, the home of renowned author Edith Wharton and her husband, Teddy, have also recently been meticulously restored to their original grandeur, as has the house itself. The gardens of these three estates are among those featured in these pages.

Nevertheless, historic gardens are just a starting point for anyone interested in seeing how the gardening tradition has flowered in the Berkshires. Contemporary gardeners continue to make the most of incomparable landscape features and to inventively tackle challenges such as lean, rocky soil and unpredictable weather.

As we envisioned this book, we decided to look for gardens that excelled on several levels. We scouted hither and yon and discovered an abundance of stunning gardens, more than we could possibly include. Ultimately, we sought gardens demonstrating exceptional design and personal creativity, responsiveness and sensitivity to a given site, and an aura of celebrating the Berkshire region.

In these pages we showcase five must-see public gardens and a diverse collection of exceptional private Edens. These great gardens range from formal to naturalistic, with many variations in between. Their size and scale also vary. Some are tended by one or two hands-on gardeners. Other properties rely on help from one or more landscape professionals. A few gardens grace the grounds of getaway houses; others surround year-round homes. In every case, we sensed a guiding personal vision that propelled the garden to a level of greatness.

The ones we chose revealed their charms time and again as we visited them at various stages throughout two growing seasons and, in some cases, in winter as well.

I offer a word here about how we define "the Berkshires." One geographical definition places the Berkshires within the approximate triangle bordered by the Housatonic, Connecticut, and Deerfield rivers. The broadest definition of the Berkshires that we found includes the area from Hudson, New York, to Woodbury, Connecticut, and north through western Massachusetts into southern Vermont. Our parameters were a bit tighter. We chose to extend slightly beyond the lines of Massachusetts' Berkshire County to encompass the topographical range of the Berkshire Hills, which extend south just into northwestern Connecticut and west into New York from Canaan to Amenia. Rich Pomerantz and I both live in lower Litchfield County, Connecticut, an area often referred to as "the foothills of the Berkshires." The hills in our respective towns, lovely as they are, don't quite measure up to what we consider certifiable Berkshire height requirements. Whatever definition you embrace, I hope you will find a fitting tribute to Berkshire gardening on these pages.

One of my goals was to unearth the personal stories of these gardens, to learn how an individual or a couple cultivated an ongoing relationship with a place that somehow translated into a garden of uncommon beauty. In researching the public gardens, certain aspects of American history became ever more alive as I explored the contributions of some major artists, as well as the overarching cultural heritage of this region.

What emerged intrigued me, especially the threads of interrelated influences and approaches to design. For example, renowned landscape gardener Beatrix Farrand designed parts of The Mount's landscape for her aunt, and Farrand also inspired John Stewart McLennan's way of designing his gardens at Ashintully. To accentuate these threads, we have included sidebars on the design influences and strategies espoused by garden makers.

We hope our presentation of great Berkshire gardens will spur you to explore the cultivated landscape gems of this region, or will intensify your already kindled appreciation of this area. Information on visiting the public gardens is included in each chapter. Among the private gardens, many are open for tours during the gardening season. The most common touring options are through The Garden Conservancy's Open Days Program (see Appendix). As we scouted for this book, we found other public gardens and places with exceptional landscapes of likely interest to garden lovers. The Appendixes briefly profile some of the most noteworthy places, listed by general geographic area as an aid to trip planning.

When we mentioned this project to friends and colleagues, the common response was "That really sounds like fun." In fact, it has been. At every turn, we encountered beauty, graciousness, and enthusiasm. Gardeners exude passion and generosity, and being in their presence or soaking up the ambience of their gardens encourages a good time. Best of all, the Berkshire region lives up to its fame. Exploring its great gardens and other treasures is an unparalleled joy. We hope this book will inspire many delightful excursions, as well as joyful and rewarding gardening. 🌿

A Rich Legacy of Public Gardens

Culture, Cultivation, and Visionary Creators

Composer John Stewart McLennan transformed a farmstead in Tyringham, Massachusetts, into an elegant garden under native maple trees. Ashintully became a public garden after his death in 1996.

THE MOUNT
The Revival of Edith Wharton's Gracious Gardens

LENOX, MASSACHUSETTS

It's often said that every garden reflects its maker. The gardens surrounding The Mount certainly convey the formalism, elegance, and grandeur that author Edith Wharton displayed in her life and writing. Born into the wealth and stature of "Old New York," Wharton moved comfortably within the social spheres of the Gilded Age, though she gradually defied some of its strictures to accommodate her imaginative spirit and keen intellect—traits not encouraged by her family or early social network. One of the most prolific and successful writers of her time, Wharton eventually relied on her literary earnings more than her inherited wealth to continue to live in a grand and gracious manner.

Edith Wharton wrote in her 1934 memoir, *A Backward Glance,* "The Mount was my first real home." It was the first and only home she envisioned from the ground up, a

Edith Wharton artfully blended formal and naturalistic elements as she responded to a magnificent hilltop site. A curving path, which features a series of grass steps, winds through a rock garden along one side of the house.

project she undertook at age thirty-nine as she was beginning to establish herself as a writer. In 1901, Edith and her husband, Teddy Wharton, chose to build their country place at the highest point of a former 113-acre hillside farm in the resort town of Lenox, Massachusetts. Working with architects and gardeners, she played out her dream of "integrating a house within a landscape," although some might argue that the white-stuccoed fifty-five-room mansion dominates the landscape. Over time, much of the view of Laurel Lake that was carefully accentuated from key rooms of the house has been hemmed in with the growth of distant woodlands, thus changing the relationship between house and site. However, with the recent revival of The Mount's gardens, including some clearing to expose part of the lake, Wharton's vision can still be readily appreciated.

Historians provide ample evidence that Edith Wharton served as a primary visionary of all aspects of The Mount, both inside and out. Among her gifts was a sophisticated sense of visual aesthetics. Her writings include vivid descriptions of landscapes, buildings, and objects within spaces. Her first book, an influential treatise called *The Decoration of Houses,* was coauthored with a friend, the architect Ogden Codman, Jr. Published in 1897, the book advocated a departure from Victorian trends of excessiveness and capricious decoration. According to Wharton, "The interior of a house is as much a part of its organic structure as the outside, and . . . its treatment ought, in the same measure, to be based on right proportion, balance of door and window spacing, and simple, unconfused lines." The book, which became a classic, has remained in print as a guide to commonsense interior design.

The Whartons worked with Codman on the initial plans for The Mount. Edith and Codman are usually credited with the idea of building The Mount directly into the rocky hillside, an inventive design that allowed the house to literally merge with its site. The seventeenth-century Belton House in Lincolnshire, England, served as an initial inspiration

for The Mount, which also incorporates influences from classical Italian and French architecture. After a temporary falling out with the Whartons, Codman disengaged himself from the project. Francis L. V. Hoppin then served as the main architect, although Codman designed some key interiors. Throughout the building process, the perfectionistic writer oversaw countless intricate details. Hoppin also lent his architectural expertise to the design and construction of the stonework in the Italian walled garden at The Mount. He and Edith reportedly enjoyed a harmonious collaboration based on a shared design philosophy.

As she was conceiving The Mount's gardens, Edith was writing essays about her travels to research Italian houses and gardens. These pieces were eventually collected and published in 1904 as *Italian Villas and Their Gardens*. Although her renown as a writer grew with the popularity of her fiction, she gained confidence and honed her craft in these earlier forays into nonfiction. The early works also provide insights into her strongly held aesthetic sensibilities. While living at The Mount, she wrote her first best-selling novel, *The House of Mirth*, which was published in 1905.

Another important player in the landscape design of The Mount was Edith's niece, Beatrix Farrand, a founding member of the American Society of Landscape Architects who became well known as a groundbreaking garden designer. Farrand (who was then

Above: Plants with strong geometric shapes contribute to this garden's crisp structure. Conical arborvitae line the walk to the sunken walled garden. **Opposite page, top:** *A Palladian staircase descends from an expansive Italianate terrace to formal gardens.* **Bottom:** *In the walled garden, sweet autumn clematis, a white-blooming vine, softens the contours of tall stone walls.*

EDITH WHARTON'S SOURCES OF INSPIRATION

Italian gardens: *"The real value of the old Italian garden plan is that logic and beauty meet in it, as they should in all sound architectural work.*

Each quarter of the garden was placed where convenience required, and was made accessible from all the others by the most direct and rational means; and from this intelligent method of planning the most varying effects of unexpectedness and beauty were maintained."

"It was the great gift of the Italian gardener to see the natural advantages of his incomparable landscape, and to fit them into his scheme with an art which concealed itself."

—**Italian Villas and Their Gardens**, *1904*

French gardens: The flower garden at The Mount is based on a seventeenth-century formal layout.

English gardens: Edith Wharton's personal library includes William Robinson's *The Wild Garden,* an influential book that touted naturalistic gardens, as well as Reginald Blomfield's *The Formal Garden in England.* Her flower garden reflects English planting styles.

New England landscapes: Edith frequently toured the New England countryside and loved discovering plants in the wild. She strived to capitalize on existing landscape features and included many regionally native plants in her gardens.

Beatrix Jones) enjoyed a lifelong bond with her aunt. She was just getting established in her career as a landscape gardener, as she always called herself, when she designed two important areas of The Mount: the maple tree allée leading to the house, and the kitchen garden. The former remains today, even grander more than a century after its planting. The latter will be revived, according to Farrand's original plan, as part of the complete restoration of the Wharton estate.

A seasonal "country place," The Mount was designed as a summer home where Edith could write and the Whartons could relax and entertain guests. The gardens were backdrops for these purposes and gave expression to Edith's passion for gardening and landscape design. From 1902 until 1911, the Whartons' estate served as a setting for spirited gatherings of Edith's growing network of artistic and literary friends, including other luminaries such as novelists Henry James and Paul Bourget. For Edith, The Mount

A shallow pool edged with low plantings serves as a focal point in the flower garden. Edith Wharton placed this sunny space on a direct axis with the walled garden, a shaded retreat on the opposite end of the lime walk.

was not intended as a showplace; rather, it was a haven to nurture her creative spirit in the company of like-minded companions. She and Teddy were known as incomparable hosts who afforded their guests exquisite hospitality and opportunities for solitude as well as conviviality. Their home's location in what was then still "the country" gave Edith the chance to observe and record natural wonders and to "hear only silence." She often spent six to seven months there, until 1911 when her husband's progressing illness led to their decision to sell the house. From then on Edith lived in France.

The Mount has two distinct types of gardens: formal and naturalistic. The straight-lined axial layouts draw the most attention, both by their prime locations as they form a cascade from a terrace that borders the house, and by the sheer power of their geometry. But Edith Wharton also valued nature's untamed beauty, with its more subtle patterns. She opted for sinewy lines and naturalistic plantings in transitional areas between

cultivated gardens and wilderness. One such planting on the north side of the house features irises, forget-me-nots, and buttercups bordering a natural stream that flows through a woodland. A massive rock garden, created around outcroppings on which the house stands, showcases many native species, including large stands of snakeroot and baneberry. Other native plants within her naturalistic gardens include trilliums, Jack-in-the-pulpit, sweet fern, ostrich fern, goldenrod, and asters. An intrepid explorer, she often dug up plants from the wild and relocated them to her gardens.

One of The Mount's most compelling design elements is a series of gracefully curving grass steps located just beneath the rock garden. Edith may have seen a turf staircase in England or been inspired by "green theaters" in Italy. In any case, the concept was innovative in North America at the time, according to Betsy Anderson, The Mount's former garden historian. Says Anderson: "Edith meant for The Mount to be an American garden,

a fusion or synthesis of garden elements from various European styles and from all points in history."

The Mount's dramatic link between house and garden is the expansive Italianate terrace that overlooks formal parterres and distant hills. Although Laurel Lake is now mostly obscured, the Whartons originally framed that vista by selectively clearing trees, the overseeing of which was one of Teddy's favorite activities. Four rooms opened onto the terrace: the dining room, the drawing room, the library, and Teddy's den. An immense green-and-white-striped awning over the center section provided shade. The terrace was used day and night for everything from reading and table tennis to alfresco meals and stargazing. From the terrace, a Palladian staircase leads to a lime walk, which links two spaces that are polar opposites in tone and style: the walled garden, with its cool shade and green-and-white planting scheme, and the colorful flower garden, which basks in full sun.

Although much of The Mount's landscape reflects Edith's fascination with Italian garden style, with its architectural masses of green, her flower garden indulged her appreciation of nature's floral exuberance. In a letter to her friend Sara Norton on July 23, 1905, Edith wrote "[My flower garden] is really what I thought it never could be— a 'mass of bloom.' Ten varieties of phlox, some very gorgeous, are flowering together, & then the snapdragons, lilac and crimson stocks, penstemons, annual pinks in every shade of rose, salmon, cherry & crimson . . . the lovely white physostegia, the white petunias, which now form a perfect hedge around the tank—The intense blue Delphinium Chinense, the purple & white platycodons, & c.—really with the background of hollyhocks of every shade from pale rose to dark red, it looks, for a fleeing moment, like a garden in some civilized climate." She effused in another letter to Norton, "I am really growing besotted about gardening."

Top: An allée of pleached lindens, known as the lime walk, adds to the strong linear structure. ***Bottom:*** Delphiniums and astilbes flourish in the flower garden. ***Facing page, top:*** Snowfall accentuates the garden's geometry. ***Bottom:*** Boxwood parterres surround a fountain in the walled garden.

Edith's flower garden was a synthesis of several types of gardens that she had seen in her European travels. The structural layout was based on a seventeenth-century French design, but the plantings are more effusive, like those in an English flower garden. The perennials and annuals were selected for their hardiness in the Berkshires. After archaeological digging and research, this garden has been reconstructed with the varieties that she planted.

Since 1980, when the nonprofit organization named Edith Wharton Restoration bought forty-nine acres of The Mount's original estate lands, the house and gardens have been gradually returned to their former splendor. (After the Whartons' tenure, the estate served as a private residence, a girls' dormitory for the Foxhollow School, and the home of a theater company.) The Mount's refurbishment sped up in recent years with the help of a $2.9 million federal challenge grant from Save America's Treasures. In addition to being open for tours, The Mount hosts events relating to literature, gardening, and history.

Top: Arching wands of snakeroot (cimicifuga racemosa) add to the garden's naturalistic style. Bottom: The flower garden's formal layout was based on a seventeenth-century French design.

Visiting The Mount Estate and Gardens

2 Plunkett Street, at southern junction of Route 7 and 7A, Lenox
413-552-5111; www.edithwharton.org

Guided tours of house; self-guided tours of garden; gift shop and cafe.
The Mount hosts events relating to literature, gardening, and history.
Open daily May through October and weekends until Christmas; hours vary.

NAUMKEAG
An Artful, Groundbreaking Collaboration

STOCKBRIDGE, MASSACHUSETTS

The hilltop gardens at Naumkeag, the Choate Estate, have achieved legendary status as iconic works of landscape art. They began to astonish visitors with their unabashedly modern design elements back in the 1930s, and they continue to garner acclaim for their inventiveness, charm, and creative use of space. They were born of a dynamic collaboration between a pioneering landscape architect, Fletcher Steele, and a well-heeled and open-minded client, Mabel Choate.

But the story of Naumkeag dates back to a half century earlier. It was built as a summer home by Mabel's parents, Joseph Hodges Choate (1832–1917), one of the most prominent Manhattan attorneys of his era, and his wife, Caroline Sterling Choate (1837–1929). Joseph served as ambassador to England from 1899 to 1905, and was close friends with President Teddy Roosevelt and writer Mark Twain. Choate also cofounded

Fletcher Steele designed the idiosyncratic Rose Garden to be viewed from above. Serpentine waves of pale pink gravel accented by roses flow within a spacious lawn.

FLETCHER STEELE'S AND MABEL CHOATE'S SOURCES OF INSPIRATION

Generalife in Granada, Spain; and French knot gardens: The Afternoon Garden's "giddy carpet," a patterned layout of shallow fountains and low boxwood, was inspired by Fletcher Steele's memories of Generalife, and by an old French knot garden.

Cubist gardens at the Paris Exhibition of 1925: Fletcher Steele attended this show featuring work by leading modernist designers. Innovative designs relied on new structural and axial principles reflected in Cubist art, and incorporated unconventional materials such as mirrors and colored gravel.

Travels to China: Both Mabel Choate and Fletcher Steele visited many gardens in China that served as models for Naumkeag's Chinese Garden, a pastiche that includes authentic elements as well as imaginative interpretations.

*Above: A circular Moon Gate serves as an entry into the Chinese Garden. **Facing page:** Lanky trunks of white birches create dramatic interplay with curving white handrails in an Art Deco feature called the Blue Steps.*

the Metropolitan Museum of Art and was a peace activist and an engaging raconteur. His wife, an artist before her marriage, continued to study art as she raised five children; she later taught art to her Stockbridge neighbors. An advocate for women's rights and education, she was a cofounder of Brearley School and Barnard College, both in Manhattan. Her daughters were two of Brearley's first five students.

Naumkeag was designed in 1885 by Stanford White, of the renowned architectural firm McKim, Meade & White. The eclectic forty-four-room shingle-style house was sited into the side of Prospect Hill above a huge oak tree beloved by the Choates. A broad open porch overlooks panoramic views of the Berkshire Hills and the sunset. The forty-nine-acre estate also functioned as a self-sufficient farm and garden that produced food for the Choate family and its staff. The house featured intricate woodwork and comfortably scaled rooms. In contrast to many ostentatious mansions of the era, this home was graciously informal and livable—a bustling family retreat rather than a showplace. Naumkeag, a word meaning "place of rest or harmony," is the Indian name for Salem, Massachusetts, Joseph Choate's birthplace.

Mabel Choate, who had summered at Naumkeag with her mother for many years, inherited the estate after Caroline Choate's death in 1929. Mabel left the property to The Trustees of Reservations, a nonprofit trust, upon her death in 1958. Mabel made few changes to the home's decor, so it retains the period flavor and artifacts of a creative and globe-trotting family. Tours provide fascinating glimpses into the Gilded Age.

Although Fletcher Steele's landscape designs put Naumkeag on the map, the grounds and gardens were initially developed by landscape architect Nathan Barrett in the late 1880s. Fletcher Steele wrote that he approved of Barrett's work and wanted to build upon the existing designs while creating new spaces. In a sense, Naumkeag's gardens represent a blending of the classical Beaux Arts style with the edginess of modernism. Among Barrett's designs that remain are a formal evergreen garden around a circular pool, an arborvitae walk, and two broad-lawn terraces, one that serves as an extension of the house. Caroline Choate designed a linden walk within the woodlands at the south end of the property, inspired by linden allées that she had seen in Germany.

The thirty-year collaboration between Mabel Choate and Fletcher Steele began in 1926 when she attended a lecture he gave for the Lenox Garden Club. She invited him to visit Naumkeag the next day and soon after they began working on their initial endeavor, what became known as the Afternoon Garden. This whimsically ornamented terrace next to the house features shallow black-glass pools and low boxwood hedges

*Previous pages: In the sculpted South Lawn, the flowing lines of embedded cedar posts emphasize the slope's contours, which echo the profiles of a distant mountain. **This page, top:** The renowned Blue Steps were designed as a way for Mabel Choate to reach her cutting garden at the base of a hill. **Bottom:** The Evergreen Garden surrounds a circular pool. **Facing page:** The rill bisecting the brick walkway flows into the same reservoir that circulates water through the series of pools within the Blue Steps.*

in an intricate pattern. The vertical structure of this outdoor room was made from old pilings dug from Boston Harbor painted to resemble Venetian mooring poles; rope garlands drape between the posts. The setting fulfilled Mabel's desire to enjoy an easily accessible outdoor room that delighted the senses and framed the distant vista.

Naumkeag's most famous garden feature is an Art-Deco–styled staircase called the Blue Steps: azure-painted fountain pools are flanked by four flights of stairs with curvilinear white rails. Set within a grove of white birches, the Blue Steps feature merges a completely original structure with spectacular plantings to create a mood of timeless abstraction. Fletcher Steele came up with the stunning design in 1938 as a way for Mabel to walk down the steep hillside to her cutting garden. A rill, which begins just a few steps down from a set of stairs leading to the Afternoon Garden, flows down the hillside into the series of pools, connecting house and landscape in subtle continuity.

Another innovative design was the "sculpting" of a hillside to create what is often considered the first modern "earthwork" in American landscape design. On the South Lawn, an undulating low "fence" accentuates the slope's graceful contours, repeating the lines of mountains in the distance. This project, which took several years to complete, grew out of Mabel's impulsive purchase of truckloads of landfill that were heaped on what had been a daunting incline.

Fletcher Steele considered himself first and foremost an artist. His passion as a landscape architect was to create "dreamscapes" for his clients. In a lecture in Westport, Connecticut, he said, "Dreaming enables us to withdraw into ourselves for brief moments and rests us. It is good and if a garden makes it easier and pleasanter to dream, then it is a good garden." He also had been steeped in the classical traditions of his profession. After two years of landscape architecture studies at Harvard, he was lured by Warren Manning to work as his assistant, a post he held for six years before going off on his own. Manning had been a protégé of Frederick Law Olmsted, often considered the father of American landscape architecture.

Mabel Choate was an avid gardener, reader, and world traveler whose hobbies included painting and collecting art. She enthusiastically encouraged Fletcher Steele in his imaginative approach to design and even designated a room for him at Naumkeag. One

of their most ambitious projects was the Chinese Garden. Steele began designing it in 1937 after Mabel's 1935 visit to China. He incorporated artifacts she brought back as well as elements of gardens she had visited. Building the Chinese Garden on a New England hillside was a challenge, but the designer and client were intent on creating something evocative and new rather than merely a reproduction. Its centerpiece is the Chinese Temple, a pavilion reached by climbing a broad staircase that faces the mountains. Another signature element is the round Moon Gate, which serves as an entry through a fern dell on one side. This Chinese-inspired garden room feels peaceful and otherworldly.

One of the last creations at Naumkeag, and perhaps most idiosyncratic, was the Rose Garden, just below one side of the house. Meant to be viewed from above, the garden featured eleven ribbons of pale pink gravel swirling across a green lawn. Roses were planted as punctuations beside the gravel paths.

Wandering through Naumkeag's eight acres of gardens provides great lessons in how different spaces can inspire a wide range of moods. The gardens also offer inspiration on the dynamic use of color, form, and texture on a grand and gracious scale. 🌿

Top: The Afternoon Garden features a patterned parterre and colorfully decorated poles.
Bottom: Floribunda roses accent the Rose Garden's sinuous paths.

CHESTERWOOD
The Sculptural Sensibility of Daniel Chester French

STOCKBRIDGE, MASSACHUSETTS

A sensational view of Monument Mountain moved Daniel Chester French so profoundly in 1896 that he immediately bought the Stockbridge farm that provided the vantage point for the vista he so admired. The celebrated sculptor settled there in 1898 with his wife, Mary, and their young daughter, Margaret, and named their summer estate Chesterwood. Its landscape became another outlet for French's creative expression for more than thirty years.

Daniel and Mary were hands-on gardeners who participated in the planting and weeding of their gardens. Daniel enjoyed choosing seeds and plants and also remained involved in the utilitarian aspects of the estate, from farming and logging operations to the roadway and drainage systems. Having grown up on a farm in Exeter, New Hampshire, he was used to tending land.

The renowned sculptor of the Lincoln Memorial designed his studio on an axis with a Hydrangea Walk that leads to the woodland garden. A display of pink and white peonies precedes the summer-blooming hydrangeas.

Above: Two Ionic columns grace an entrance to the woodland garden. ***Facing page, bottom:*** *A walkway bordered by plantings leads from the house, at left, to the courtyard outside the studio, which includes a curved marble bench.* ***Top:*** *In the perennial border, spikes of hollyhock blooms tower over a mound of yellow coreopsis.*

In 1901, the Frenches tore down the farmhouse and replaced it with a seventeen-room home that was comfortable and modest compared to other "summer cottages" of the era. French also designed a large studio to accommodate his massive sculptures in progress, and he worked there from late spring to fall. An innovative railway track running from inside to outside the studio afforded the easy movement of work to observe how shifting light affected its appearance.

Daniel Chester French's best-known sculpture is the evocative seated Abraham Lincoln that graces the Lincoln Memorial in Washington, D.C. He developed the piece at Chesterwood, and models for it are on view in his studio. He also sculpted the famous Minute Man monument in Concord, Massachusetts, which was his first commission, in 1873 when he was only twenty-three years old. His commissions for public sculpture numbered about a hundred.

Daniel designed both formal and informal gardens at Chesterwood, which began as 83 acres and eventually encompassed 165 acres. A remarkable aspect of Chesterwood is how artfully the studio and its surrounding gardens are blended into the site and relate to the adjacent woodlands. The same principles of proportion, scale, and form that informed the artist's sculptural work guided his garden designs. A pergola structure, located along a hemlock hedge west of his studio, was placed to frame the spectacular mountain view while providing an intimate sheltered nook. The Frenches often enjoyed quiet afternoons there. Other aspects of the formal garden include a long border facing the studio, and a curved seat known as an exedra, which faces a fountain that Daniel designed in the studio's entry court.

On a direct axis from the studio entrance and exedra, a short stairway leads to the Hydrangea Walk, which continues as a path into the woods. Within the woodland, French created an extensive path system that was punctuated at key points with scenic overlooks and other destinations. He spent many hours plotting these refinements to the woodland with his lifelong friend William C. Brewster, an ornithologist and writer from Concord, Massachusetts. One area, the Hemlock Glade, is a circular clearing with benches and stylized plantings of species that thrive in shade, including native maiden-hair fern and mountain laurels. Another enchanting space, called The Circle, features a

DANIEL CHESTER FRENCH'S SOURCES OF INSPIRATION

Classical Italian gardens: The pergola and axial layouts are examples of Italian-inspired design elements. French studied art in Florence for two years as a young man and remained enamored of Italian classicism.

Charles Adams Platt, a garden designer, inspired the Frenches with his garden in Cornish, New Hampshire, that seemed to them "a kind of American Italy."

English landscape design: Chesterwood's long border reflects the flower garden style popularized by Gertrude Jekyll. French's extensive library includes books by William Robinson, who promoted naturalistic gardens.

American ornamental farms: French cultivated Chesterwood as essentially an "ornamental farm" in the spirit of Monticello and Mount Vernon, striving to make it both funtional and beautiful.

An entry garden connects the sculptor's studio with an allée called the Hydrangea Walk, seen here in bloom. French designed the circular fountain that is the courtyard's centerpiece.

marble-and-cement seat adorned with female Greek sphinxes that Daniel designed. He created the space, which originally surrounded a large sugar maple, as a play area for his daughter and her friends. Although the maple is no longer standing, the setting still conveys a wondrous merging of formality within the natural terrain.

The house was designed with two porches and a gravel terrace to serve as extensions

of the living space. Daniel's studio included a massive rear porch facing Monument Mountain. The Frenches often hosted parties where he displayed his work in progress, and they held festive costume balls under Chinese lanterns. Among their circle of friends were artists, actors, and writers, including and Edith and Teddy Wharton when they lived at The Mount, in nearby Lenox. Daniel eventually designed several gardens

Above: A long border showcases sun-loving perennials. ***Facing page:*** *Pink peonies (top) golden-petaled black-eyed Susans, globe thistle, and flowering tobacco (bottom) are among the summer bloomers.*

*Top: Within the woodland, a space called The Circle features a bench designed by French. **Bottom:** Rick Brown's wood-and-steel sculpture titled* Regeneration *was part of the annual "Contemporary Sculpture at Chesterwood" exhibition during 2006.*

for friends as an unpaid consultant. As he did with Chesterwood, in each case he created intricate models of the site as part of his planning.

Margaret French Cresson lived at Chesterwood after her parents' deaths, then bequeathed the property to the National Trust for Historic Preservation. Chesterwood offers valuable insights into Daniel Chester French's artistic sensibilities and glimpses into the country life that he and his family enjoyed. The Barn Gallery, on the property, showcases a portion of what may be the largest body of work by any American sculptor. Expanding on the use of this landscape as an outdoor gallery for contemporary sculpture, Chesterwood hosts an annual exhibition in the woodland. Contemporary works are chosen and sited by a different curator each year. It seems a fitting way to draw visitors again and again to a landscape that is both breathtaking and subtle.

Daniel Chester French once wrote, "I think the test of a garden is whether you like to be there, and whether you feel like staying and enjoying it, instead of wondering at its magnificence." Chesterwood clearly passed that test. It remains an enchanting landscape garden that invites strolling and lingering. ❦

Visiting Chesterwood

4 Williamsville Road (off Route 183), Stockbridge
413-298-3579; www.chesterwood.org

Guided tours of the house and studio; self-guided tours of the gardens. Exhibit gallery, museum shop, and picnic area. Public programs throughout the year include antique car and carriage shows, bronze-casting and marble-carving demonstrations, an outdoor contemporary sculpture exhibition, and lectures and family activities on sculpture and architecture. Open May through October, daily 10–5.

ASHINTULLY
A Symphony on the Land

TYRINGHAM, MASSACHUSETTS

Frederick Law Olmsted once wrote: "Landscape moves us in a manner more nearly analogous to music than anything else." Considered the father of American landscape architecture, Olmsted strived to create spaces with musical qualities such as variations on themes, flourishes, and a rhythmic sense of movement.

The gardens at Ashintully, in Tyringham, Massachusetts, embody a subtle and haunting musicality. They were created by John Stewart McLennan, an accomplished composer of contemporary classical music and film scores. A self-taught gardener starting in midlife, he wove a series of imaginative vignettes on about four acres of undulating terrain around a 1785 farmhouse. Mature deciduous trees, especially sugar maples, create soothing shade and a sense of grand scale for this mostly green landscape garden. Hundreds of acres of meadows and mountainous woodlands, which have been preserved as open space, form dramatic backdrops and extend the garden's vistas.

In 1965, the year before John McLennan married Katharine White Bishop, he began his garden by planting a formal layout of arborvitae trees near the house. He continued to mastermind and cultivate the interconnecting spaces and settings until shortly before his death in 1996. At that time, the property was given to The Trustees of Reserva-

A slender fountain in a former cow pond serves as a dynamic focal point within this landscape garden. It can be enjoyed from many vantage points on the sloping site.

BY DESIGN

JOHN STEWART McLENNAN'S SOURCES OF INSPIRATION

Beatrix Farrand's designs at Dumbarton Oaks: As a child, McLennan often visited his godmother, Mildred Bliss, at her estate in Washington D.C. when Beatrix Farrand was installing the renowned garden there. Years later, he used Farrand's technique of creating full-size mock-ups of garden structures, then moving them until they were in the right place. Ashintully's gardens also artfully blend classical embellishments with natural land contours, one of Farrand's signature design achievements.

Historic European gardens: The McLennans visited many gardens in Europe and were especially inspired by those in England and Italy. Seeing an extraordinary

continued on next page

*Above: A brick-floored formal room provides a shaded respite. A statue of Eleanor of Aquitaine holds a place of honor. **Facing page:** Moss-covered stone walls beneath ancient maples imbue a sense of timelessness.*

tions, a Massachusetts-based, nonprofit land trust, subject to the life estate of Katharine.

A garden often reveals a subtext beyond its overt structure or planting schemes. The story of Ashintully began some fifty years before John McLennan began cultivating the land. Ashintully, completed in 1912, was originally the thousand-acre estate of Robb de Peyster Tytus and his wife, the former Grace Seely Henop. They named their thirty-five-room Georgian mansion Ashintully, which means "on the brow of the hill" in Gaelic. It was designed by Francis L. V. Hoppin, the architect for The Mount, the Wharton estate in nearby Lenox. A year after the couple moved in, Tytus died. His widow, a noted linguist and writer, went on to marry John Stewart McLennan, a Canadian senator, newspaper owner, and historian. Their only child, John Jr., was born in 1915.

Young John McLennan endured a series of devastating losses. His parents separated when he was two and his father returned to Canada. His mother died when John was thirteen; he learned of her death at boarding school by seeing an article in a newspaper as he was polishing his shoes. His half-sister, Mildred Tytus, ten years his senior, then became his guardian. She died in a car accident when John was eighteen, and he moved to Canada and reconnected with his father. Katharine McLennan said her husband benefited from finally getting to know his father for a few years before the latter's death. "His father was a wonderful man, so he had that," she said. In 1937, young John McLennan pur-

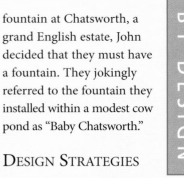
fountain at Chatsworth, a grand English estate, John decided that they must have a fountain. They jokingly referred to the fountain they installed within a modest cow pond as "Baby Chatsworth."

DESIGN STRATEGIES

Let a site guide a design. John McLennan told writer Randall Howe: "The pleasure one gets is from ordering, not subduing, nature . . . the marvelous potential lay of the land, that's my excitement, that's what's compelling." John did not consciously replicate design elements. Instead his gardens evolved "organically," one phase after another, based on what seemed to work best with the site.

Create interplay between opposites. Ashintully exhibits dynamic relationships between wild and cultivated elements, light and shade. Spatial variations range from intimate enclosures to wide vistas.

chased his family's former summer estate. The mansion proved difficult to maintain as a year-round home, having been designed as a summer place. In 1948, John moved to the estate's farmhouse and converted the hay barn into his music studio. In 1952, the Ashintully mansion burned in a forest fire triggered by drought. All that remained were the foundation, the front terrace, and four Doric columns. Katharine McLennan, commenting on her late husband's history, said, "You don't want to read too much into these things. But my feeling of why it was so important for him to make something beautiful was because of this incessant loss."

When John McLennan began tackling the old farm site, it was completely overgrown with weed trees and underbrush. In an article about the garden in *Berkshires Week* in 1988, John is quoted as saying he had no master plan and that his garden took shape "all by eye." He progressed "step by step, with many missteps," by clearing one area at a time, visualizing possibilities, then making a few preliminary sketches. Katharine says he "took out what he didn't want and left what he did." He pored over books about gardening and garden design and paid special attention to sight lines, axes, proportions, and creating a balanced sense of layering—from the treetops and hillside to ground level. He focused on spatial relationships and on designing a journey to be enjoyed from more than a dozen seating spots. Although Katharine McLennan modestly declines any credit for the garden's

Above: John McLennan's musical sensibilities are apparent in the rhythm of his garden layout. The site's hilly terrain and native trees guided his designs. ***Facing page, top:*** Embellishments include a wrought-iron gate with a floral motif. ***Bottom:*** Four Doric columns on a terrace are remnants of the former Ashintully mansion.

design, John is quoted in several articles as relying on her keen eye and sense of proportion.

Ashintully melds formality and naturalism with creative aplomb. John McLennan often placed a symmetrical pair of objects to mark an entry or adorn a sitting area, imbuing the garden with a timeless sense of order. He also paid homage to the asymmetric sculptural qualities of the natural terrain. He used stone walls and other structures to accentuate existing land contours rather than modifying the challenging terrain, thus evoking a lyrical, flowing ambience. He heightened the impact of stately, immense native maples by pruning their lower limbs. The banks of the brook that intersects the garden remain rugged, providing a stark contrast to the garden's formal qualities and groomed lawns.

John's artful managing of space reflects a clear vision and steady restraint. He indicated paths within broad swaths of lawn by simply mowing the grass in a different direction, thus creating uncluttered spans of "negative space." He planted trees, shrubs,

and ground covers to heighten spatial relationships. He used few flowering perennials; instead, he placed pots with annuals as formal accents, and deliberately limited the color palette.

John worked out the placement of permanent objects, such as urns, statues, and pillars, by making cardboard mock-ups, then moving them around and assessing them from various vantage points (see sidebar, page 38). His use of ornament was elegant and understated. A classical urn on a pedestal atop a knoll embodies both majesty and stillness. Placed at the highest point of this landscape, the urn draws the eye from numerous viewing points, serving as a kind of visual touchstone. After walking up a dramatic moss-covered stone staircase to the pedestal, a visitor is rewarded with another layer of meaning: an inscription that reads "Sweet day, so cool, so calm, so bright. The bridal of earth and sky." The quote is from a poem by seventeenth-century English metaphysical poet George Herbert.

An intuitive, fluid approach to design is evident in what John McLennan created

Top: *A footbridge designed by John McLennan crosses a natural brook, exemplifying the juxtaposition of cultivated and untamed elements in this garden.* Bottom: *Classical ornaments direct the eye and mark points of passage.*

over three decades. His carefully orchestrated garden journey offers intriguing perspectives and distinctive episodes to savor along the way. It's easy to imagine how he might have sensed the flow of this landscape in musical terms. One key repeating element is the presence of water. He transformed a cow pond by adding a fountain with a dramatic vertical spray. A counterpoint to this flourish is the subtle sound of a burbling brook spanned by two footbridges that he designed, along with the garden's walls, steps, gates, and patios. His helpers in executing these projects were members of the Loring family, from Tyringham and Otis.

Katharine finds it telling that her husband knew when he had completed his landscape garden. "It was about a year before he died, and he was in good health. When he said 'I've finished the garden,' I told him that was ridiculous—a garden is never done. But he said 'No, I will not add any more areas, though I may do some refinements.' He felt satisfied with what he had achieved."

In 1997 Ashintully received the H. Hollis Hunnewell Medal, established in 1870 by the Massachusetts Horticultural Society to recognize gardens of country residences embellished with rare and desirable trees and shrubs. McLennan's work as a composer was recognized with an award from the American Academy of Arts and Letters. His legacy of Ashintully Gardens affords glimpses into the spirit of a man whose passion was cultivating beauty. ❧

Visiting Ashintully

Located at the intersection of Main and Sodem roads, in Tyringham, Massachusetts.

Owned by The Trustees of Reservations. The farmhouse remains a private residence but the gardens are open to the public. When visiting, it's worth walking the steep half-mile trail to the original Ashintully mansion, now part of the five-hundred-acre McLennan Reservation. The ruin offers an evocative glimpse of a Gilded Age relic and a sensational view of the Tyringham Valley.

Open June 1 to October 15, 1 to 5 Wednesday and Saturday. To arrange guided tours for groups, contact The Trustees Western Regional Office at 413-298-3239; www.thetrustees.org

BERKSHIRE BOTANICAL GARDEN
A Multifaceted Community Gem

STOCKBRIDGE, MASSACHUSETTS

The Berkshire Botanical Garden rests on the bedrock of years of collective effort and commitment. In contrast to the other public gardens featured on these pages, all of which were created to enhance private residences, this garden emerged on a grass-roots level to meet the needs of a regional community.

The seed idea for the organization was planted by members of the Lenox Garden Club in 1934; they also enlisted support from other nearby garden clubs and local groups. First named the Berkshire Garden Center, the botanical garden initially served as a resource for gardening in the Berkshire region and as a gathering place for gardeners. A resident horticulturist was hired in 1935 to design a trial garden and share gardening advice.

Bernhard and Irene Hoffmann donated the garden's original six-acre site after an initial trial year for the project. The property included a 1790 farmhouse, now called the

A grass path winds through the de Gersdorff Perennial Garden toward the Center House.

THE HERB ASSOCIATES:
Camaraderie in the Garden and Kitchen

On any Tuesday morning from April through October, you're likely to encounter a group of avid volunteers called The Herb Associates tending the Herb Garden or making herbal concoctions in the adjacent Center House kitchen. This group of mostly women began gathering in 1957 to create herbal products as an ongoing fund-raising effort. The Herb Associates line features mustards, dressings, jellies, vinegars, and dried herb seasoning mixes, which are sold in the BBG gift shop and at the Harvest Festival. One of their products is an herb mustard based on a secret recipe that is guarded by one person at a time, an honor that has been held by only three of the associates.

Many Herb Associates remain active for decades. Gertrude Burdsall, one of the three founding members, continued as a guiding force until she died in 2006, just shy of her hundredth birthday. Her friend Emily Rose (see page 53) was another founder. Currently about twenty associates share knowledge and story-telling as they labor side by side. They work in teams in one of four locations: Gardeners tend the herbs in the dis-

Fresh chives are prepared for an herbal concoction.

Herbs dry on screened racks.

An Herb Associate pours salad dressing into bottles.

play garden and a supply garden; another group preserves herbs in the drying room; and the kitchen crew cooks and bottles the products.

Center House, which continues to serve as a hub for meetings and other activities. Themed gardens were planted around the building and gradually throughout the site; one of the first projects was a border of native shrubs along the roadway. The Hoffmanns also donated a second property with a house that now serves as the Visitor Center.

Among this garden's historic treasures is the Herb Garden, designed in 1937 by landscape architect Edward F. Belches. A rocky slope was transformed into a charming niche for varieties of hardy and tender herbs displayed in stone-terraced beds according to use, plant family, and ornamental value. This garden has been tended for more than a half century by devoted volunteers called the Herb Associates. A shed next to the garden became a resource library, with plant references, cookbooks, and displays on methods of drying herbs. Today, exhibits in the shed feature the individuals who nurtured this special garden and reveal the generous spirit of this place.

In 1941, a thirty-by-one-hundred-foot demonstration garden was planted to show how a modest plot could produce vegetables for a family of three for summer use, canning, and winter storage. The following year the center became involved in the national Victory Garden Program popularized during World War II. It added a Youth Garden, a planting of fruit trees, and classes on nutrition and canning.

Over the years, the center grew to encompass fifteen acres. It was renamed the Berkshire Botanical Garden (BBG) in 1991. Its horticultural displays now feature more than three thousand species presented in many gardening styles and habitats. Each area is designed to inform and inspire home gardeners about planting and growing techniques, design concepts, plant selection, and, in some cases, ecology. For example, the Wetland Garden demonstrates how a catch basin can be planted with native species to remove pollutants from runoff water before it descends into the soil to become ground-

Above: Low stone walls form raised beds in the Proctor Garden. *Facing page, bottom: Hen-and-chicks grow on a miniature "green roof" in the Children's Garden.*

Previous pages: Sixteenth-century limestone balls grouped on a rock outcrop were part of a 2007 exhibition on ornament in the garden curated by The Elemental Garden of Woodbury, Connecticut. **Above:** *The historic hillside Herb Garden showcases edible and medicinal plants.* **Facing page, top:** *An Herb Associate harvests basil in the Herb Garden.* **Bottom left and right:** *Daylilies and hardy geraniums are among the abundant bloomers.*

water. The Vegetable Garden showcases about eighty varieties of vegetables, herbs, and edible flowers, all grown organically. Some are heirloom varieties passed down for generations. A new Children's Garden, with its imaginative plantings and whimsical structures, encourages youngsters to develop a passion for nature. Nearby, a storage shed is adorned with a huge window box lushly planted with annuals.

These varied garden spaces can also be enjoyed simply as a beautiful backdrop for a leisurely stroll. There are sunny borders and shade gardens, an impressive rock garden on a jutting outcrop (created by the Berkshire Chapter of the North American Rock Garden Society), and a shaded pond garden with a waterfall. Some areas showcase collections of roses, hostas, daylilies, primroses, and native plants. A passive-solar greenhouse built into a hillside demonstrates an energy-saving design with water barrels and a brick floor. A larger greenhouse features tropical and desert plants and is open to visitors year-round.

Display gardens are open seasonally, and horticultural and environmental programs occur year-round. In addition to its lecture series and hands-on workshops, the BBG offers a noncredit horticultural certificate program for professionals and home gardeners who want to systematically expand their skills and knowledge base. The program is conducted jointly with the Massachusetts College of Liberal Arts.

A popular Berkshire tradition since 1935, the Harvest Festival at the Berkshire Botanical Garden draws as many as 15,000 visitors to its plant sale, exhibits, and entertainments. Scores of area businesses and organizations as well as the BBG faithful (up to four hundred volunteers each year) participate in the early October weekend extravaganza. This fund-raiser is just one of the many events and programs hosted by this small garden that makes a big impact. A two-day spring plant sale is another popular event. Held since 1977, it ranks as one of the longest-running plant sales in the country. Visitors are encouraged to bring a picnic and explore spring wonders in the gardens, including late-spring bulbs, primroses, and lilacs.

Maintained by a small staff, the BBG also engages hundreds of volunteers to tend the gardens, conduct tours, and work in the office and the gift shop and on community events. It's that enthusiastic energy of pulling together and sharing knowledge and experience that makes the Berkshire Botanical Garden sparkle as a special gem.

Visiting Berkshire Botanical Garden

Located at the intersection of Routes 102 and 183 in Stockbridge.

Open 10–5 daily, May through mid-October. Educational programs are held year-round; off-season the Rice Greenhouse, the solar greenhouse, and grounds are open during daylight hours. Group rates and guided tours available with advance reservation. Facilities are available for private events.

413-298-3926; www.berkshirebotanical.org

At Little Sutton, a fieldstone wall separates
cultivated landscape from open meadow. This
private garden in Alford, Massachusetts, is
among many that feature regional materials
and honor their site's innate topography.

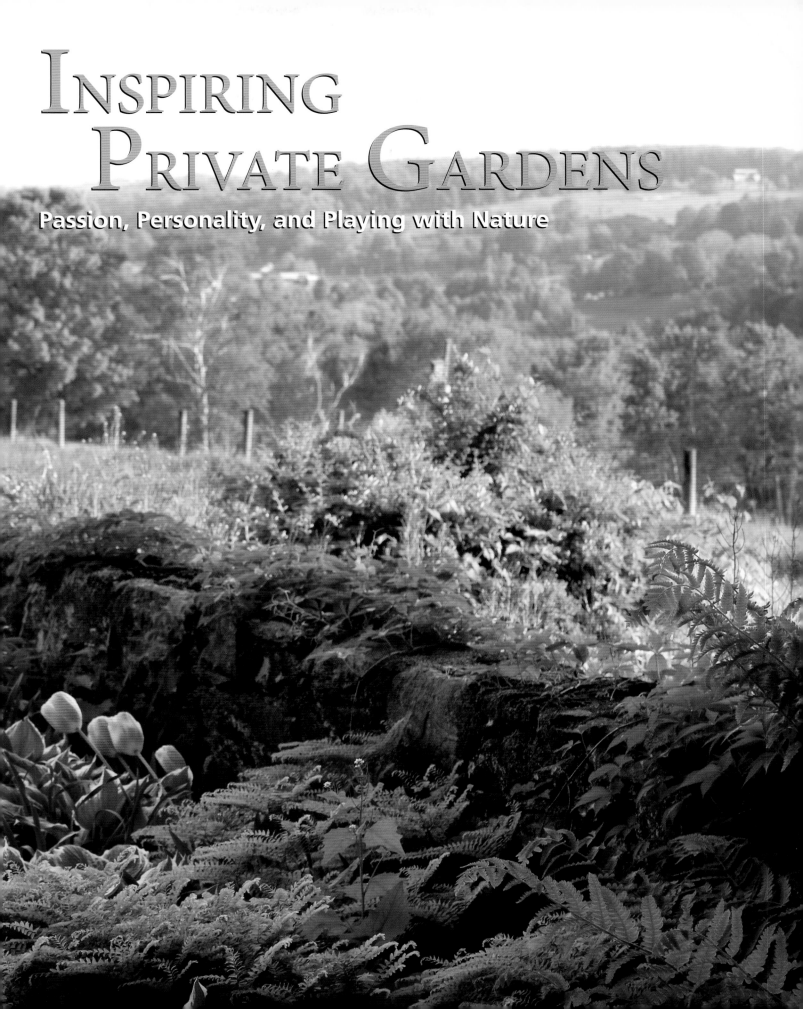

INSPIRING
PRIVATE GARDENS
Passion, Personality, and Playing with Nature

LITTLE SUTTON
Emily Rose's Garden of a Lifetime

ALFORD, MASSACHUSETTS

When Emily Rose and her family moved in 1941 to the summer home they had built on old farmland, the first garden that Emily planted was a large vegetable plot to provide sustenance during wartime shortages. The following year she installed a square herb garden near the house. Nearly a decade passed before Emily began to envision in earnest the ornamental gardens that now surround her year-round abode on a mountaintop estate.

One flowering treasure that did make it into the ground early on at Little Sutton was a wisteria vine planted at the southwest corner of the house. "We bought it at a roof sale at Bloomingdale's in 1939!" Emily proudly recalls. Over time, many structures were built to support the bulk of the vine. A sporadic bloomer for many years, the wisteria in its old age now reliably flaunts glorious purple flowers that drape from a sturdy arbor.

A venerable wisteria vine weaves through an arbor and bears profuse purple blooms. This terrace is one of several garden spaces that connect directly to the rambling house.

EMILY ROSE'S SOURCES OF INSPIRATION

Adelma Simmons, legendary expert on herbs: "She ran a nursery called Caprilands Herb Farm, in Coventry, Connecticut, where she gave yearly luncheons and invited anyone interested in herbs. I learned so much from spending time there and from reading her books. Besides information on growing, she told what herbs are named for saints and angels and such, and all their uses. It was part of my education in that world."

Berkshire Botanical Garden's Herb Associates: "There are so many dedicated herbalists in that group. I guess I eventually became one, too. I can't remember anymore all that we did."

EMILY'S DESIGN STRATEGIES

Rely on vertical elements and height variations. "I like the interruption of space with tall things in a landscape. I also like layering plantings."

Connect house and garden. "The Massachusetts Horticultural Society came to visit many years ago. They were so serious, but they gave me an award. They said how the gardens were so closely knit to the house. I've tried to make sure there's something interesting to look at from every window."

Emily Rose easily deserves the designation "legend," but in her unassuming manner, frequently peppered with hearty laughter, she shrugs off the term. At ninety-nine, she remains actively engaged with her garden even though she no longer physically tends it. (Monica Fadding, of Marconica in Glendale, Massachusetts, coordinated the garden's maintenance from 1994 until her sudden death in 2006. Since then, the garden has been maintained by her husband, Marc Fadding.)

As we sit on a small hidden terrace overlooking a spectacular view of Mount Everett, Emily contemplates what she might do with the space where a massive weeping willow suffered major storm damage and was removed. "I guess things have to change over the years. I'm growing older and so are the trees," Emily muses. Though she misses her beloved willow, which the family planted in 1958 on their oldest son's twenty-first birthday, she revels in how the sweeping view of the distant Berkshire Hills has been opened up. She also joyfully ponders possibilities for reinventing this area of the garden. "I've been sitting and looking at the view to get myself used to the space," she says. "I am thinking of making this area an 'Ode to Granite.' Of course you know how stony it is around here, so I'd like to have an exhibition with some of these old stones."

Touring Little Sutton inspires Emily to offer commentary full of wonder and fond reminiscences about specific plants and the evolution of garden spaces. She and her late husband, Milton, enlisted landscape design services for key areas, but Emily's vision for the garden has always been a driving force. "This garden grew out of the site. We could only work with what the land gave us." Milton, a lawyer based in Manhattan, was a supportive participant in landscape planning until he died in 2003. They planted most of the trees on the site, which now in their maturity create shade and architectural presence. Emily describes in vivid detail how one of the mature trees, a huge Norway spruce, made "a big symphony in the wind" outside her sitting room as she ate breakfast recently. (Her youngest son, architect Jonathan H. Rose, of Hanover, New Hampshire, designed this barrier-free addition that opens to a bluestone terrace in 1997.)

The gardens flow with an undulating rhythm that reflects the property's sloping contours. "When we built the pool, we saw that the land there formed a big curve. The earth spoke to us," she explains. So they mimicked the curve in crescent-shaped beds and steps that lead down to a circular landing. Among the few straight lines in the garden are low

fieldstone walls that serve to define lawn terraces descending from the rear of the house, and another wall that creates a border separating the main gardens from a meadow running through the valley below. Although Emily had not originally studied the concepts of the British landscape gardeners (who sought to design an entire landscape as a picturesque garden), Little Sutton took on those qualities through her intuitive response to the site. There's a sense of easy and understated elegance.

*A curving path (**above**) and a circular stone landing (**top left**) follow the contours of this mountaintop site. **Top right:** An herb terrace is bordered by lilacs and accented by white irises. **Facing page:** Emily Rose chats with the author in a nook called the Blue Café, an overlook that enjoys a grand vista.*

To counterbalance the vast openness of much of this awe-inspiring landscape, several spaces offer intimate enclosure. The Herb Terrace, just outside the door to the kitchen, is the first garden room a visitor encounters from the driveway. Surrounded in part by a hemlock hedge and French lilacs, this garden grew out of Emily's passion for herbs. Designed in 1961 by E. Gillette "Bud" Wilcox of Stockbridge (who also consulted on several other garden areas), the sheltered nook includes a dining area and a lathe house with built-in seating. (The original design had a second lathe house at the entrance, which eventually deteriorated and was replaced by a dining table.) In May the mesmerizing perfume and diverse colors of lilac blossoms, from white to dark purple, provide a heady spectacle. Later in the season, senses are delighted by the fragrances, subtle colors, and flavors of many herbs: thyme, chives, sage, marjoram, oregano, tarragon, basil, lovage, parsley, sorrel, spearmint, fennel, rosemary, bay, lavender, and bee balm.

Emily's love of herbs also led her to become one of three founding members of the Berkshire Botanical Garden's Herb Associates in 1957 (page 44). As she takes in the scene, Emily remarks, "You forget, when you start a garden, how luxuriant it can become. When the hemlocks got so big, we had to let some air in, so we pruned them up." The result is a type of peek-a-boo screen.

Another gathering spot, the South Terrace and an adjacent covered porch, features an outdoor fireplace that has been much used over the years. The fieldstone patio is planted with a yellow creeping sedum that stays neat without mowing, creating a casual, natural look. However, the sedum flowers are so fragrant that they draw swarms of bees, so the plants are given a timely trim. The terrace is bordered with low fieldstone walls and is edged with roses and a row of grape hyacinths.

One of Emily's favorite nooks is the Blue Café, named for the bright blue table and

A hand-built ceramic pot serves as a dramatic focal point on an expansive deck that overlooks the swimming pool on one side and a vast Berkshire vista on the other.

Top: Tulips and alliums make appealing companions. Bottom: An intimate courtyard features a high-backed aqua bench. It's one of several garden spaces that connect directly with the house.

two chairs nestled in a lookout with a west-facing panoramic view. Sheltered by a massive 'White Lace' hydrangea and a mature white fir, it has long been a favorite place for teatime or cocktails.

A ceramic artist for four decades, Emily loves to include pots and sculpture at strategic points in her garden. Each work of art conjures a story of how it came to enjoy a place of honor. One of the most striking pots is a huge hand-built piece that she made with her friend Olivia Stokes Dreier. It draws the eye to a corner of a deck that overlooks the swimming pool. Together with a small square succulent garden next to a wooden bench, the elements work together to create a compelling and contemplative scene.

Sitting at one of the many cozy places to rest in her garden, Emily remarks, "What a nice place this has become. It's full sun, though it's absolutely enclosed." Then she chuckles and says, "I'm old enough that now I can admire my own garden. I do that constantly, Deb, don't I?" she asks her live-in companion. As Debra Fox confirms that fact, Emily continues to bask, adding, "But I can't take credit for anything in the natural world." This part of the garden is one of the scenes that Emily plans to paint in a watercolor class being taught for a small group that meets at her home. This new venture is just another way for her to enjoy the gardens that she has nurtured for more than six decades. ❧

A Warm Palette in the Garden
Thomas Gardner's Rustic Eden

RICHMOND, MASSACHUSETTS

Thomas Gardner has created rambunctious gardens where vegetables, fruits, herbs, and flowers intermingle with ease. These gardens, behind his rambling eighteenth-century farmhouse, merge productivity with beauty, and exude a casual country flair that seems emblematic of the Berkshire region.

Tom relies on a lively color scheme in his gardens. A palette that features red, orange, and yellow echoes the brick red and mustard gold of the exterior of his house. As a result, there's a dynamic and harmonious merging of house and gardens. His explanation of how he achieved this level of synchronized color is simple and direct: "Red and yellow are my favorite colors, so I just decided to stick with them, along with orange. Then when a bit of blue or purple is added to the mix, it really stands out."

The impact of this cheerful scheme starts in spring with displays of red and yellow

This garden's fiery color scheme repeats the farmhouse's mustard and brick-red hues.

GARDENING TIPS FROM TOM GARDNER

Build the soil with organic matter. Working lots of manure into the soil helps to keep it fertile without using additional fertilizers. Gardner's compost includes aged manure, a by-product of raising poultry and sheep on his farm.

Train vines on twine. Zigzagging lengths of twine from a horizontal header to a similar footer is an easy way to grow vining plants.

tulips along with daffodils. It kicks into full throttle by midsummer. When the wonderland of color bursts into full bloom, it looks like an Impressionist's dream. From crimson and scarlet to burgundy, from apricot and peach to fiery orange, from buttery to bright yellow, the hues simmer and sizzle. Tom acknowledges that when a pink bloomer finds its way into this garden, it's usually by accident. Tom sticks to his chromatic guns.

In his main garden, Tom made a series of terraced beds that cascade along a hillside behind the house. "It started with just two borders and a grass path between them, and then I just kept going," he explains. Now there are eight parallel paths with wide beds on either side, including a path beneath a long, freestanding pergola. Up and down the hillside, paths lead to unending discoveries of intriguing perennials and annuals interplanted with tomatoes, basil, carrots, beans, and countless other vegetables and herbs. Raspberry canes that produce fruit in shades of red and peach are trained along low fences and other supports. A few apricot and peach trees are interspersed within the beds. Cherry red climbing roses tower over the back perimeter. Tom continually likes to try new and unusual plants, including perennials that are rated for warmer climates than his USDA Hardiness Zone 5 garden.

Tom encourages verticality in his structured but informal gardens. Plants ramble and clamber onto fences, arbors, and other structures. "I like things that climb," he

explains. "I plant pole beans rather than bush beans; you don't have to bend over to harvest them. How hard is that?" A nine-foot-tall pergola in the main garden area provides support for several varieties of beans, grapes, and annual vines, and it shades summer lettuces and herbs. Other plants just get tall on their own, such as sunflowers and amaranth, a statuesque annual. A metal archway allows cucumbers to scramble skyward.

The rustic character of this garden is carried out in the consistent use of simple unpainted picket fencing. Again, Tom let a motif take hold. "I started by enclosing the back garden and then it just made sense to use the same fencing in other places." Picket fences also define various rooms. A shaded front yard showcases mostly shrubs and offers several seating areas. Two other areas away from the house function as more traditional vegetable gardens for space-hungry crops such as corn and squash.

Parallel to the road, a strictly ornamental border runs along the fence for 150 feet

*Above left: Tom Gardner relishes blooms in shades of red, orange, and yellow, including scarlet bee balm and fuchsia phlox. **Above right, top and bottom:** Variegated lily flowers display a dazzling color harmony. A border along the road showcases multitudes of lilies in midsummer. **Facing page:** A multilevel stone terrace bridges the house and garden.*

The early-spring show flaunts sweeps of daffodils *(above)* followed by masses of orange
and yellow tulips *(left)*. The June spectacle
includes Asiatic lilies *(top right)*.

*Top: Grass paths provide access to the gardens on the terraced hillside. **Bottom:** Raspberries are among the many fruits and vegetables Tom Gardner grows.*

in a gently curving line. In peak bloom, this border can slow traffic along the busy thoroughfare. In spring it features bulbs and perennials in blues and yellows—daffodils, grape hyacinths, and forget-me-nots. In summer it comes into even more dramatic flourish as a showcase for lilies. Again, the color scheme is primarily hot shades of reds and yellows interspersed with whites and accented with an edging of low-growing blue lobelia. The robust limbs of an ancient crabapple extend through the pickets; Tom carefully prunes the tree to keep it from overtaking the fence or hogging the show.

Another purpose for all the fencing is to keep Tom's dogs out of the garden. He breeds Australian shepherds and Italian Meremma sheepdogs and may have up to twenty dogs at any given time. He also raises poultry and Cotswold sheep, so this twenty-two-acre working farm teems with activity. These enterprises are in addition to the family business that Tom runs, mostly from home.

This lived-in country garden also includes a series of stone terraces along the back and side of the house. Designed to incorporate multiple levels, stairways, and even a built-in bench, the exquisite stonework by Ben Cortis, of Lenox, serves as a transition between house and garden. Used often for relaxing and entertaining, the terraces and a long open porch offer views of the colorful garden panoply on the slope behind it.

Tom designed all the gardens since moving to the property in 1989, and he tended them alone until 2000, when Peter Martins, Jr., came on board to serve as caretaker and gardener. Now they plan the garden together, and Peter starts a host of plants from seed. It's part of his job to make sure the color palette remains intact. 🌿

FOLLOWING A VEIN OF LEDGE
Ian and Madeline Hooper's Rockland Farm

CANAAN, NEW YORK

A whale-shaped rock outcropping serves as the backdrop for a whimsical bench in a garden that celebrates stone.

S erendipity often fuels garden making. Ian and Madeline Hooper can vouch for that. The imaginative and extensive gardens that weave around their once-derelict Federal-period farmhouse evolved with little overt strategy, at least in the beginning. "It was all higgledy-piggledy," says Madeline.

After gazing for years at the dense forest and scrub behind their weekend home, they begin to dream of having some sort of ornamental garden on the site. Neither had much knowledge or experience with gardening, so around 1990 they brought in landscape designer Fred Callander, who lives nearby, to help them get started.

Ian says that Fred was surprised they wanted a garden set so far back from their house. That bit of forethought resulted from the couple's desire to eventually expand the house toward the rear of the property, which they did. Fred thoroughly reviewed the site

IAN AND MADELINE HOOPER'S SOURCES OF INSPIRATION

Ian's mother, the late Moira Wharrad: "She had a beautiful garden in Surrey, England, and was very knowledgeable. When she visited us, she researched all the existing plants on our site and suggested what we could do with them."

Fred Callander, a landscape designer and nursery owner in Chatham, New York: "He cleared the scrub in front of the house and made it a lawn and then designed our first garden area. His initial concept for our site and his enthusiasm were very inspiring."

Ruth and Leon Bach: "We met them when we were just starting to garden. They created their garden in Spencertown, New York, all by themselves on a very tough site and made us believe we could do it, too. Every time they visited us they brought plants, and they still do. We try to carry on that generosity."

continued on next page

Above right: After exposing the rock ledge within their dense woods, Ian and Madeline Hooper planted atop and around the ancient stone. **Lower left:** *Sweeps of grasses, daylilies, and astilbes add wispy drama.* **Lower right:** *Spiky and flowing plants emerge from an Arts and Crafts–era pot on a pedestal.*

and designed a modest island bed that incorporated the "vein of rock ledge" he discovered running through the hilly woodlands.

The garden they now call "Fred's Bed" relied on rugged perennials, such as hostas, astilbes, and spotted dead nettle clustered in sweeps. "By the time he started planting, I was out there digging with him," recalls Madeline. The bed's organic shape, a result of following the irregular lines of ledge, became their model for future garden making. Explains Madeline: "We knew we wanted a country garden that was not highly formal. It made sense for this site and also for our personalities and the way we live." Although they eventually added some structural elements with more formality, the rambling gardens feel casual and welcoming. A leisurely stroll through the site reveals surprises around every turn and plenty of enticing places to sit and take in a scene, whether in the enclosed vegetable garden or under an arbor festooned with vines.

During their early years of gardening, Ian and Madeline spent time on weekends digging in the dirt to shift gears from their fast-paced lives in Manhattan. When they sold their public relations firm in 2005, they moved to Rockland Farm full time. Since

Hortulus Farm, in New Hope, Pennsylvania—the gardens and nursery of Renny Reynolds and Jack Staub: "The vision for their garden is so personal that no one else could have created it. It's also such a big part of their lives. When longtime friends are so keen on things and take you under their wing, it empowers you."

Gardens at Great Dixter, Sussex, England: "From the first time we visited, we thought it was a special place. Years later, we were able to go there to work for a week when Christopher Lloyd was still alive. We also got to know Fergus Garret, who is continuing where Christopher Lloyd left off. We were just spinning. They were real gardeners and got their hands dirty. We learned so much from them about the passion and pleasure of gardening on a large scale. And they were happy to educate us on every detail, down to the proper way to stake plants."

then, both have become indefatigable hands-on gardeners who relish working side by side on projects day in and day out through the entire growing season.

Once bitten by the gardening bug, each gravitated toward a specific aspect of the process. Madeline discovered that she loved selecting plants and planning for their placement by visiting nurseries and poring through catalogs and reference books. Ian began walking the property and daydreaming about potential garden spaces within what was mostly scruffy woods. Says Ian: "I tend to focus on the big picture and spatial relationships within the garden." Madeline recalls their daughter's comment about his early explorations of the property: "Daddy's out looking at trees."

As they thinned trees here and there, they began to fall in love with their site's natural assets, especially all the rocks, the rolling terrain, and some venerable maples that add stature and an appealing canopy. Following their vein of ledge led them to more earnest clearing and to creating other planting beds. Neither ever dreamed that eventually they would cultivate about seven acres of gardens; their mutual passion simply fueled one project after another.

One way they have managed gardening on a large site has been to plant in masses, often by dividing plants, then relocating the divisions to another area. Massing also increases the visual impact of plantings and helps to foster a balanced sense of scale.

Above: A functional stone well makes watering easy and draws attention to the intersection of paths within the fenced vegetable garden.
Facing page: The colors and textures of rugged perennials blend with the shapes and striations of ledge stone. ***Previous pages:*** The Hoopers transformed a once-dense woodland into an undulating expanse of gardens.

*Top: A tiered fountain serves as the centerpiece of a formal terrace. **Top right:** Bronze-leaved coral bells link harmoniously with a bronze-surfaced bird bath. **Bottom:** A stone stairway melds into a steep slope.*

One of their most ambitious efforts has been to gradually transform a broad span of ledge into a steep hillside rock garden that runs 450 feet and rises to about 30 feet. Liz Toffey, a gardening friend, got them started around 1992, when she began coming one day a week to weed the outcrop's crevices and fill pockets with good soil topped with pea gravel. Although this project is still in process, it's already a jaw-dropping *uber* rock garden that celebrates stark terrain and plants that thrive there. In another part of the garden, a smaller section of ledge that spans a mere fifty feet also showcases rugged plants that thrive amid stone. Madeline loves to think of the rounded smooth surface of the back side of this ledge as her "whale."

Few individuals garden on the scale of the Hoopers, and they are quick to acknowledge their helpers. Around the year 2000, their gardening gained greater momentum when they hired their young neighbor, Mark Whiteman. He has since helped them with masonry and other landscaping projects, including a gently curving stone stairway that leads up a hillside to a garden overlook. They credit Mark's creativity, bold thinking, and problem-solving skills with spurring them to "really get serious" about their garden. Other garden helpers are Joanne Keller and William Gomez.

"We enjoy working as a team with all these talented and dedicated people," says Madeline. "It's fun to think about our garden the way we used to think about our business." Ian adds: "We have lots of frontiers, things we want to do with this site." Madeline describes one of their rituals during the temperate season. "We love to walk around the garden together when we finally quit working for the day. We might be dripping with sweat, but we just enjoy seeing everything that's happening." ❧

BALANCING VISTAS AND INTIMACY
Lee Link's Garden

SHARON, CONNECTICUT

Sites that face spectacular vistas can evoke a sense of wonder, but too much vastness can feel overwhelming. Lee Link has accentuated breathtaking views by creating sheltered spaces from which to enjoy them. "I want to feel like I'm in my garden but also protected within this big landscape that still feels a little wild," Lee explains.

Lee moved to this weekend getaway with her husband, Fritz, and their son in 1980 and soon after began "messing around" in an existing vegetable garden far below the house. She soon realized that she wanted her gardens closer by, for convenience and because she wanted to view them from indoors. "It was a hippie house," she says of the rustic A-frame built in 1970. The Links have since expanded it with additional rooms and porches that look out over White Hollow Valley's rolling hills, which are covered by fields and woods.

Simple lines of a rustic fence echo the clean shape of the stone-bordered pool, which overlooks an expansive Berkshire vista.

LEE LINK'S SOURCES OF INSPIRATION

Naumkeag (see page 21): "Mabel Choate must have been quite a fabulous character to have gone for the edgy designs that Fletcher Steele came up with, like that weird rose garden. I've also gotten a lot of ideas by how they handled their hillside site, which is similar to mine."

Innisfree: "What I love about this garden is that it's not about perennial borders. They haven't messed it up with too much planting. It's basically a green landscape garden and brings design right down to the basics. They've done a major amount of editing and have also manipulated natural water features so well. Yet I know that creating something simple can be complicated."

Helon Dillon, Irish gardener and author: "I attended a lecture

continued on next page

An existing low stone wall had defined the lower edge of what became terraced gardens. Lee had additional parallel walls built to anchor perennial beds and a long rectangular water garden. "I had to do something to make this steep hill feel less daunting," she says. The perennials beds, planted in a palette of burgundy, purple, yellow, and chartreuse, rise up with feisty plants that command attention. Another compelling goal was to make the tall house, which is set on a hillside, seem less imposing. She planted two hornbeams on either side to frame the house.

A key lookout onto Lee's perennial borders is a large porch with screens on three sides. The spacious, comfortably furnished room also offers views of an outdoor terrace next to the porch with a shade border behind it and the valley in the distance. (Eventually the Links bought a neighboring tract so they could edit trees in the foreground to see this vista.) On the lower level of the house, a sleeping porch off the master bedroom makes a

where she said she got sick of the face of her house, so she planted some birches to screen it. I realized that's what I could do with our former garage (now a guest cottage), which I always hated. So I planted four birches in front to soften the building. Michael Trapp helped me to come up with a design."

DESIGN STRATEGIES

Use architectural plants to make a statement. "When you have a lot of space, you need bold plants, not 'wussy' ones. I like plants that are tall, that have big leaves or strong lines. I'm especially crazy about agaves and other succulents, and *Verbena bonariensis.*"

Repeat a design element. "I like round things, so I have a lot of objects and plants with orb shapes in my garden."

cozy haven for napping or reading. "You're really in the garden there," says Lee. Next to the porch, an arbor draped with wisteria and grapevines serves as a shady plein air spot to relax.

Over the years, Lee has spent a lot of time just looking at parts of her landscape trying to figure out what might work. "I think design is something that takes time. I guess I have an eye," she reluctantly admits, "but it's much harder to work with space in a garden than it is with interior rooms." She credits the insights of friends and fellow gardeners, especially Bunny Williams (an interior designer) and Michael Trapp (an antiques dealer who also designs interiors and gardens). Lee took inspiration from Michael's garden in West Cornwall, Connecticut, to create the Old World style of her courtyard. "I also love to visit gardens and go to lectures; that's how I get a lot of ideas."

Lee weaves complex elements so adeptly that their placement seems effortless and

*Center image: Two olive jars diagonally punctuate the border of the sleek swimming pool. Blooms of giant alliums **(above)** and sculpted corbels and finials **(far left)** bring other spherical elements to this garden.*

even inevitable. That's the case with diverse plantings and with objects, from massive urns to orbs of various sizes. This easy elegance has apparently been hard won. Lee admits to agonizing over the placement of objects, acknowledging that she's had nearly three decades to work things until they feel right. "None of this happened in one fell swoop," the self-taught gardener asserts.

The property includes numerous garden spaces, but Lee deliberately keeps a significant amount of the landscape open, either with meadow or lawn. "I love the negative space of the country. I try to respect that," she says. When they added a pool, Lee made sure that it was tucked in a corner of the property so as not to become a focal point in the landscape.

Although the plantings in this garden appear lush, an underpinning sense of restraint pervades. One bed below the screened porch is planted with a long swath of Russian sage. The simple design showcases the freewheeling drama of the leggy stems swaggering their purple wands of bloom. Another planting along the stairs to a greenhouse makes an olfactory statement as striking as its visual impact. Lavender stalks rise up and enchant a visitor, encouraging a slow ascent to savor the profound fragrance. To add to the visual dazzle, Lee plants the self-seeding annual *Verbena bonariensis;* its purplish flowers on lithe stems look like baubles as they "dance" above the lavender. Behind

This page: *More spherical shapes accent the water garden and the garage with its circular window.* ***Facing page:*** *Shade plantings around an outcrop convey an easy sense of naturalism.*

the greenhouse, a terraced garden relies on masses of low-growing perennial grasses.

Lee Link walks the tightrope between whimsy and understated formality in her garden. How does she manage the delicate balance? "Well, you have to have the courage of your convictions," she says with a chuckle. "You just have to go with it. I don't like to plan everything out. In the spring I like to just go out and plant a lot of different things. But I also try to edit. I stand back and sometimes I say to myself, 'What was I thinking?' I move things a lot. Also, I try to keep it country, and not too highfalutin'. You can get too uptown. I really feel like I'm in the country here."

Because the rear of the property rises up steeply with dense woods on ledge, a less ambitious gardener might have left well enough alone. But when Lee learned that a nearby nursery closing its doors was unloading its hostas for a dollar a plant, she bought a truckload of them and started planting at the base of the slope. Eventually this mostly

Top left and above: A dining porch overlooks a bed filled with statuesque plants. ***Lower left:*** Succulents add sculptural impact in a rustic still life. ***Right:*** A glazed pot planted wtih succulents enjoys pride of place in the entry courtyard.

shaded border extended the full length of the cultivated part of the property and merged subtly with the untamed woodland. She likes the quiet mood of this mostly green garden that is accented by bits of yellow foliage and blooms.

Although she has part-time help, Lee spends many hours tending her gardens and thinking about how to improve them. Acknowledging that gardens are always in flux, Lee is contemplating a drastic makeover of her perennial garden. "I'm tired of flowers. I think they're overrated," Lee says, following the comment with hearty laughter. "I'd like to be able to simplify things and maybe make it a little edgier." She pulls out a simple pencil sketch of a layout that relies heavily on trees with underplanted perennials. "Will I have the courage to do it? That's the question," she muses. Given her track record of trying new things, it seems likely that she'll go for it. 🌿

In her greenhouse, Lee indulges a passion for sculptural plants.

GOOD DOGS FARM
Maria Nation Weaves Tales in her Garden

Grass paths wend through billowing displays of perennials, shrubs, and ornamental grasses.

ASHLEY FALLS, MASSACHUSETTS

The urge to garden awoke in Maria Nation only after she bought an old farmhouse on eight acres in 1996. Then the urge took hold with a vengeance: "The act of gardening came naturally to me because I have a tolerance—perhaps a love—of hard work, nurturing, and being in the dirt and sweating," she explains.

Maria's gardens wrap around the house, the garage, and a small barn, and extend down into a four-acre field that abuts the Housatonic River. They exude whimsy, exuberance, and intrigue. Working at home as a screenwriter for television dramas, Maria knows how to spin a good tale. Her garden making likewise gets fueled by narrative. "I ask myself, 'What is the story for this space?'" she explains as she takes me along a series of meandering paths.

In creating what she calls her "yurt"—a garden focal point that immediately catches

my eye upon entering her backyard—the story was simple. "I grew up in California and was used to living outdoors. I wanted to sleep outside, so I ended up building this little getaway." The room conveys romance and rusticity. A gauzy mosquito net is draped above the bed, and there are windows on all sides. A clear crown of glass affords a view of the night sky. She and her partner, Roberto Flores, sleep in the yurt all summer. Along the turf grass path leading to the sleeping room are billowing mounds of purple-flowering catmint, ornamental grasses, and hydrangeas.

To further fulfill her desire to live outside, she also created an outdoor shower, cozy niches for relaxing and entertaining, and most recently an outdoor bake oven. She obsessed for months on the oven's design, researching many options and structural issues. Eventually she enlisted Mark Mendel, of Monterey Masonry, a brick mason and writer whose attention to detail and love of storytelling matched hers. She shows off the animal paw prints and other anomalies in the reclaimed nineteenth-century bricks and antique marble cobblestones. "He had been saving these for years waiting for some special project," she says, delighted by the additional layers of meaning imbued in the structure. Once the oven was completed, she made a room around it by planting a fast-growing hedge of variegated Japanese willow. This space is just one of several intimate rooms within her garden.

Another chapter in Maria's garden evolved as a way to honor the memory of her mother. She had planted a circle of fourteen fruit trees—pear, apple, and plum—with an allée leading to this orchard. She later found an egg-shaped stone that seemed like the perfect memorial and placed it at the center of the circle, above where her mother's ashes are buried. She loves the dynamism of the circular space and how it frames a view to the sky. "There's no marker or anything, but I know what it means to me. In writing, there are times when the writing gods or the unconscious or whatever it is just hands you the

Above: Deep-pink lilies take center stage. *Top:* A gravel walkway leads to a seating area surrounded by exuberant plantings. ***Facing page:*** Sweeps of purple catmint line the approach to an outdoor sleeping room.

Top: *An iron horse head marks the entry into an area that includes a mass planting of self-sown 'Hopi Red Dye' amaranth.* **Above:** *Spring bloomers include magenta peonies.* **Right:** *Plantings that form lush layers of texture and color invite exploration and screen the freestanding garage.*

MARIA NATION'S SOURCES OF INSPIRATION

Barbara Bockbrader, garden designer, floral arranger, and owner of Campo de' Fiori in Sheffield, Massachusetts: "Barbara was the first person to give me permission to trust myself as a gardener and just go with my instincts. Her gardens are full of small discoveries and surprises. They have an organic romanticism and continue to inspire me. I always drop by when I'm stuck or discouraged."

Michael Trapp, antiques dealer and designer of gardens and interiors: "Michael's garden in West Cornwall, Connecticut, is one of my all-time favorite places. You are transported to another universe through a small portal. To call it a garden doesn't do it justice. He has created a place that juxtaposes beauty and decay, life and death, past and future, sadness and ecstasy. It's everything a garden should be—absolutely personal, built by one's own hands, and expressing some intangibility beyond shrubs and flowers."

DESIGN STRATEGY

Garden for yourself. "This sounds easier than it is. It requires being conscious of who I am and what I am doing. This slow process of analysis and self-reflection then unfolds into what the garden becomes, and it fulfills something on a deeply personal level."

perfect bit of synchronicity. I actually put in the orchard before my mother died, not knowing that the circle of trees would create this powerful dynamism. Then my mother died and I realized that I had unconsciously built a perfect memorial for her."

As Maria's intuitive garden design process unfolded, she experienced fits and starts. After she initially planted with abandon, she felt that the garden's design was not cohesive, but did not know why. She struggled to figure out why she was gardening in the first place, among other big questions. That's when she started planning out her pathways in advance. "Barbara Bockbrader, a garden designer, suggested that I figure out where I wanted to go within the property and then mow a path there." That bit of advice led to ripping out the entire garden she had planted and starting over. "Then I began to understand why people kept telling me that structure needs to come first, then planting. Now it seems obvious, and I can't even think about plants until I build the structure— the path, the wall, whatever."

There's another reason for all the interweaving paths in Maria's garden. "I so wanted to be in the garden and not just looking at it," she explains. "At one point in Hollywood there were movie theaters with what was called 'Sensurround,' with seats that wobbled and sound all around. I wanted my garden to feel like that—dramatic and intense."

Says Maria with a chuckle, "There's nothing too subtle about me. This garden reflects that." Yet there is much subtlety to discover in this garden: intricate detailing in the way entries are marked with unusual found rocks and other ornaments, and planting combinations that display carefully planned gradations of harmonious color accented by pleasing contrast, and variations in shapes and textures.

Maria compares the process of designing a garden to painting and sculpting. "But it's like sculpting a moving target in the dark. You plant something and then you have to wait to see how it will grow in your garden and what the real color of the blooms will be and how they look next to what else you've planted. And then you hope it does the same

Above: The outdoor bake oven, where Maria Nation bakes artisanal breads and pizza, anchors a dining courtyard. *Facing page:* Maria tends her kitchen garden with her standard poodles in tow. A rustic Chippendale-style fence encloses the space.

Top left: Maria uses an antique rake to harvest chamomile flowers. Right: Purple irises and pink flowers of beautybush (Kolkwitzia amabilis) bloom together in June. Bottom: A Mexican ceramic pot at a main entry is among the objects that adorn Maria's gardens.

thing the following year. Gardening, I've discovered, is more about faith and hope than control. But now I appreciate that I can't control it. I just have to go with it, see what happens, and then work with that."

Maria gradually discovered the value of shrubs in her garden. Not only do they hold their place better than the constantly shape-shifting perennials, they provide the "gravitational pull" that anchors the beds. Increasingly, flowering perennials are becoming more incidental as she is drawn more to interesting foliage in burgundies and chartreuse, soft blues, and gray greens. If the plants flower, too, so much the better. Her newest garden, a room beneath the canopy of a venerable maple, relies on two brow-shaped borders that feature a variety of shrubs, including variegated dogwood and dark-leaved ninebark.

Besides her extensive ornamental plantings of perennials, shrubs, and trees, Maria tends a large kitchen garden. Bordered by a rustic cedar Chippendale-style fence, this garden does double duty as another destination. Flowering perennials adorn the crop rows, asparagus plumes disguise a cedar-clad outdoor garden sink, and a "secret" room bordered by sunflowers hides a small fire pit to sit beside on cool evenings.

From the vegetable garden, a wide central walkway leads to a meadow through which extensive paths are mowed to offer more options for excursions. One path leads to the Housatonic River, where a pair of Adirondack chairs serves as an intimate perch. Maria and Roberto especially enjoy this prospect at dusk, where they often share tales of the day 🌿

CULTIVATING SIMPLICITY
Nancy McCabe's Garden

FALLS VILLAGE, CONNECTICUT

Nancy McCabe thinks a lot about the concept of simplicity. Her garden reflects that preoccupation, even though there's plenty happening here.

This site harmoniously interweaves many utilitarian elements within a flowing landscape that is all about beauty. From the driveway, visitors enter a small kitchen garden enclosed by tall espaliered apple trees through which massive stone outcrops can be glimpsed on one side. This dynamic tension between structural formality and nature's rugged contours continues throughout Nancy's garden. Herbs, vegetables, and hot-colored annuals grow within neatly structured beds bisected by brick paths and edged with antique scalloped tiles. Bell-shaped glass cloches, used early in the season as miniature greenhouses, are placed artfully as a trio within one bed. A metal bench next to the house and an Adirondack chair off in a corner each invite lingering,

Clipped boxwood "buttresses" contribute to the structure of the sunken garden. A metal lantern, one of three, hangs from a saucer magnolia.

Nancy McCabe's Sources of Inspiration

Gardens at Paca House, a historic estate in Annapolis, Maryland: "I always loved the way the gardens descend from the house as terraced rooms that can be seen from different perspectives. That's what I wanted to achieve on a small scale with our sunken garden. Making a flat space out of what had been a crumbling hillside was a challenge, but I finally figured out how to make it work."

French country houses: "I went to school in France and always admired the simplicity of the architecture and how houses and gardens are related. When the back porch on this house needed to be replaced, a fieldstone terrace seemed more appropriate. Aromatic herbs such as thyme now grow between the stones, a look that's popular in France."

Design Strategies

Less is more. "I'm always promoting the idea of restraint when I work with clients. Sometimes you have to pull back and reduce the elements competing for attention and not plant in every available space. The eye needs places to rest in a garden."

Relate your garden to your life. "If you harvest green beans from your garden and then cook them, it means something as you eat them. I love to use a certain copper basket made by Mayo Indians. It's sturdy and useful and beautiful and is part of the whole process of enjoying everyday activities."

especially at dusk when the enthralling scent of Mexican jasmine perfumes this outdoor room.

From the kitchen garden, a rustic cedar arbor leads to other gardens. Close to the house, several structures are dynamically integrated within the landscape: a potting shed filled with terra-cotta containers in intriguing shapes, a chicken coop with a charming cupola, and a rustic clothesline structure that is much used. An open terrace along the back of the house offers spaces for dining and lounging. It's bordered on one side by a small greenhouse that Nancy's husband, Mike, built next to the kitchen.

The centerpiece of this backyard landscape is a large sunken garden that can be viewed from various vantage points. Bordered by a hillside and a low wooden fence, this garden's structure includes clipped boxwoods that resemble buttresses. As one enters this room, the eye is drawn to an old French stone slab table and a set of American iron chairs.

"This garden used to be more floriferous," explains Nancy, "but now I like the soothing quality of green more." The space is certainly not without color or interest, however.

Throughout the growing season, a variety of trees, shrubs, and perennials take turns in starring roles. Hellebores, one of Nancy's favorite plant groups, subtly shine in spring, interspersed with low boxwood. In early summer, the white burst of blooming *Crambe cordifolia* makes a dramatic statement, along with lilies, peonies, and brown-and-caramel-colored iris. In August, the large purplish flower clusters of Joe-Pye weed are harmoniously linked with a burgundy-stemmed snakeroot and 'American West' lilies, which sport a hint of burgundy in their buttery-yellow petals. The late-summer show includes the white blooms of a 'Tardiva' hydrangea, 'White Profusion" butterfly bush, and datura, followed by the attractive and edible fruits of medlar and quince.

Views of distant massive trees are framed by the layout, and a woodland serves as a

Left: In August, a corner of the sunken garden features a harmonious combination of tall 'American West' lilies and Joe-Pye weed blooms. Top: White-blooming Crambe cordifolia *shines in a bed adorned by a fanciful sculpture. Bottom: Antique tiles, originally from Georgia, line brick paths in the kitchen garden.*

Above: An Adirondack chair provides a place to pause in the kitchen garden. Facing page, left: The wall enclosing the sunken garden was stuccoed to repeat the surface of the house. Right: An elegant pot on a pedestal creates interest along a passageway. Bottom: The chicken coop and rustic clothesline were designed to be beautiful as well as useful.

majestic backdrop for the entire garden. Three metal lanterns hang from a mature saucer magnolia and provide appealing diffused light at night. A low, round carved-stone birdbath rests beneath the magnolia tree just above one upper corner of this garden; another stone birdbath, an old English pig trough, is tucked within the sunken garden, creating a subtle relationship between recurring elements.

As a counterpoint to the straight-lined geometry of the sunken garden, winding paths lead strollers through a stylized woodland garden. Here, granite outcrops have been exposed and accentuated, and plantings favor sweeps of loosely shaped boxwoods, as well as ferns (maidenhair, cinnamon, ostrich, and Christmas), hellebores, Solomon's seal, and periwinkle. Along the way, visitors may be enticed to sit for a spell on an old joggling board from South Carolina, a long seat that slopes toward the middle, making it popular with courting couples. The house and other structures are visible in the

Top: Espaliered apple trees form a see-through screen around the kitchen garden. ***Bottom:*** *A weathered peacock trough looks at home in this country garden.*

distance as one returns from the woodland, sited in pleasing rapport with one another. The stucco walls and wooden stairs of the sunken garden mimic house materials, creating the sense that the garden was once somehow part of the architecture. (The eighteenth-century farmhouse was originally wood sided; stucco was added about 1900.) That persistent attention to detail and the repetition of materials and elements foster the simple seamlessness that pervades this garden.

Nancy McCabe's cultivated hillside, with views of distant hills across the road, showcases her holistic approach to design. About half of the two-acre site is gardened; the rest is untamed woodland on a steep hill along one side of the property. Since moving to the neglected property with her family in 1980, Nancy has let the house and site inspire her. "I am always driven by the architecture," the longtime garden designer explains. "I was originally drawn to the plainness of this house, and have tried to make gardens that suit it." Often she has let the plantings themselves serve as adornment, such as the four espaliered pear trees in front of the house, and arbors with climbing vines that grace two doorways.

In Nancy McCabe's world, simplicity seems to refer to the process of paring things to an essence and integrating elements in ways that appear inevitable and elegant. She says this garden suits the low-key lifestyle that she and Mike and their two sons have lived over the years. There's an aura of serenity in this garden, and an atmosphere that embraces all the everyday pleasures of home. 🌿

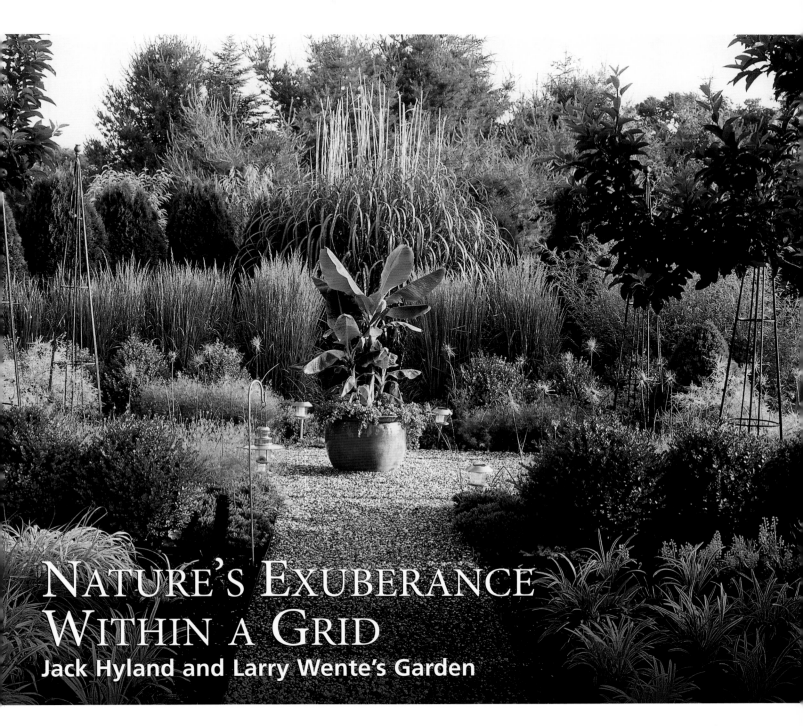

NATURE'S EXUBERANCE WITHIN A GRID
Jack Hyland and Larry Wente's Garden

MILLERTON, NEW YORK

A s a gardening duo, Jack Hyland and Larry Wente rely on different skills and inter-
ests, but they share an overarching vision. When they bought a forty-one-acre site
in the midst of hilly farmland, they wanted to make a house and garden that blended
harmoniously into the surrounding environment. They did just that—exquisitely—on
many levels.

Larry, a Manhattan-based architect who specializes in "green" buildings, designed
the contemporary house and several modest outbuildings to conjure the spirit of indigenous farm structures. Jack, an investment banker and avid plantsman, focuses on plant
selection and overall garden maintenance. Together they've created a distinctive getaway
that interweaves formal and informal elements.

"This house is meant to feel informal, like a modern version of barns built in this

*A blue-glazed pot brimming with hefty
banana plants draws the eye down a
gravel path.*

BY DESIGN

JACK HYLAND'S AND LARRY WENTE'S SOURCES OF INSPIRATION

Villa Lante: "This great garden, located between Rome and Florence, depends almost totally on structure rather than on flowering plants. It starts at the top of a hill, looking almost primordial, and becomes gradually more elaborate and formal. At the bottom of the hill, the garden sweeps around two small pool houses and connects with the living space. For a public garden, it's very human scaled."

Villa Gamberaia, in Fiesole, on the outskirts of Florence: "This is an apotheosis of a private garden. You go through a high wall of cypress, and then are confronted by open space on one side of the villa, with wonderful views of Florence. After winding around the main villa, you come upon the gardens on the

continued on next page

area," explains Larry. "During the seventeenth and eighteenth centuries, farm buildings had a haphazard quality in how they were placed, so this house is asymmetrical to reflect that." He also made sure the house was laid out to merge with the landscape. One of their favorite spaces in every season is a sitting room that can be open or enclosed; it juts into the landscape and offers breathtaking views through windows on three sides.

There's also a strong rectilinear formality in the layout of this house and garden. Both were designed using four-foot modules: Nearly all indoor and outdoor rooms are sized in multiples of four. For example, garden spaces are eight feet by twelve feet or twelve feet by sixteen feet. All the paths are four feet wide. Architecturally, a key reason for this approach is practical: It makes construction more economical. "Most building materials come in dimensions that are multiples of four, such as four-by-eight-foot sheets of drywall, paneling, and insulation," explains Larry. He adds that this attention to proportion is also satisfying on another level: "The logical mind recognizes that there's something orderly about the structure. Even if you can't articulate it, you can feel it."

Although the garden encompasses only about a quarter acre, long and narrow axial views make it seem bigger. Sight lines extend from points within the house all the way down paths to focal points at the far end of the garden. The house was also designed to take advantage of spectacular "borrowed" scenery beyond the property: Indian Lake and rolling hills with fields and woods. Views of the surrounding open landscape, which vary dramatically from different vantage points, are framed through windows that selectively limit specific vistas.

Jack notes that an iconic barn on a distant hillside looks almost Japanese. To connect the house with this vista, he and Larry planted a meadow with timothy grass and native wildflowers. They mow the meadow twice a year to keep it from becoming overgrown with scruffy trees. Visitors are drawn into this larger landscape by way of curving mown paths.

far side. They are a series of discrete beds linked to each other. The real beauty is that nothing is gigantic. We loved walking around them."

Fernando Caruncho, a Spanish landscape designer: "We saw a garden in a book on his work (*Mirrors of Paradise: The Gardens of Fernando Caruncho*) in which he had planted a meadow with cypress and olive trees in a patterned layout. We can't grow cypress but we can grow *Chamaecyparis* (false cypress), and we planted apple trees instead of olives. Then we underplanted our little orchard with low grasses."

Piet Oudolf, a Dutch garden designer: "He's big on native plants, all-season interest, and creatively mixing textures, colors, and forms. We have one specific bed next to the garage that we call our homage to Piet Oudolf."

One design challenge of a large site is how to make a garden that is not dwarfed by the surrounding panorama. That was one of Larry's concerns. "When you have a huge, open site, how do you make a garden that can compete with that scale? Our solution was to make big blocks of plantings; you have to create a large-scale statement. That's the hardest thing to get right." Many of their garden beds are divided into four-foot-square planting areas. These grids are planted in bold blocks of individual plants, monochromatic groupings, or some other scheme such as culinary herbs. Within the grid of this garden, the moods of various spaces change in large measure by the variations among the plantings. For example, one tucked-away niche with a bench is surrounded by tall bamboo, which adds to the contemplative atmosphere. There's a sense of discovery as you stroll from place to place.

Jack and Larry's bold and effusive planting style deliberately pushes against the underlying geometric grid. Regionally native plants are featured prominently, including many types of perennial grasses. These free-spirited plants relate to the surrounding landscape and are in keeping with Jack and Larry's desire to emphasize ecological habitats in their garden. Another dramatic environmental feature is the prominent placement of cobalt-colored solar panels at ground level within the garden. The angled panels, which generate much of the house's electricity, look like contemporary sculpture: "We thought we would expose them rather than hide them," says Jack. "The color is very rich. The way the light hits the crystals changes the intensity of the color." In late summer, the panels are accented by masses of black-eyed Susans. Other ecological features include a system to recycle graywater from the house for use in the garden, and cisterns that capture rainwater for irrigation.

An aspect of their efforts to create balanced scale includes emphasis on vertical elements. Tall conical evergreens and an arbor contribute to the garden's year-round

Top: Stately 'Karl Foerster' grasses frame a view of the pool. ***Above:*** *A delicate* Allium schubertii *bloom resembles a starburst.* ***Facing page, top:*** *Long sightlines create connections between house and garden.* ***Bottom:*** *Masses of variegated hostas and 'Sweet Kate' spiderwort create rhythmical symmetry along a sky-reflecting rill.*

Top left and right: Within the house, a long hallway with glass doors at either end aligns with one of the main garden paths. ***Bottom and facing page:*** Textural plantings soften the strong lines of the axial layout. ***Previous pages:*** The garden merges into the surrounding landscape. Behind the outbuildings, banks of solar panels add sculptural interest.

Top left: Larry Wente sweeps a garden path.
Right: *Low lanterns light the paths.* ***Lower left:*** *Like punctuation marks, slender obelisks and a tall* tuteur *add vertical structure.*

backbone, and husky perennials rise up to make seasonal spectacles. Twelve stately *tuteurs,* each holding a reflective gazing globe, make a memorable statement in a planting bed close to the house. These whimsical-looking ornaments evolved serendipitously. Larry intended the *tuteurs* to support vines and be lit from below at night. The globes, added as focal points for the uplighting, keep the light from dissipating into the darkness and reflect sunlight by day as well. There are also many plants with round elements in this garden, because Jack is especially fond of umbel flowers such as Queen Anne's lace and the spherical blooms of alliums, globe thistles, and sea hollies.

Although Jack spends much of every weekend in the growing season tending the garden, he and Larry also rely on gardener Deborah Davidson to help maintain the intensely planted beds. One aspect of working within a well-defined structure is keeping everything in balance. Whereas Jack is often tempted to try new plants and fill beds to the brim, one of Larry's favorite activities is "editing" the garden. That push-pull process seems to contribute to the garden's dynamic allure. ❦

A FORMAL COUNTRY GARDEN
Bunny Williams Creates Many Moods

FALLS VILLAGE, CONNECTICUT

Opposites attract, the adage goes. Opposites can also make well-suited bedfellows in a garden. That's part of the allure of the series of outdoor rooms that surround the weekend home Bunny Williams shares with her husband, antiques dealer John Rosselli. Here you'll find classical statuary and neatly clipped boxwoods as well as roaming chickens and plantings that seem to jump with joy.

A renowned interior designer based in Manhattan, Bunny Williams often blends eclectic elements from different periods to create cozy and dynamic rooms. Her gardens also juxtapose varying styles and moods, heights and shapes, and—most of all—materials. Her book entitled *On Garden Style* has become a classic reference for creatively using structure, materials, and design principles in garden making.

Not surprisingly, Bunny's gardens encompass a series of clearly delineated rooms

The parterre garden showcases colorful masses of annuals planted within clipped boxwood grids.

BUNNY WILLIAMS'S SOURCES OF INSPIRATION

Old Westbury Gardens, Long Island, New York: "It's one of the world's great, great gardens, and you don't have to go very far to see it." Walking under the covered walkway in this garden inspired Bunny to build a pergola in her own garden.

English gardens: "Cranborne Manor in Dorset is one of my favorite gardens; it's just magic. It has everything—formal gardens, a vegetable garden, a woodland garden. Lady Salisbury [Marjorie "Mollie" Olein Wyndham-Quin] first gardened there before she went on to become the mistress of Hatfield House. I've also been inspired by the gardens at Hidcote and Sissinghurst."

DESIGN STRATEGIES

Leave openings in enclosed spaces. "It's important to have more than one doorway in a garden room, so that you can see beyond into another space. It feels less confining and creates intrigue about what comes next."

Tie the style of a fence to a building. "What's the feeling you want to create? For a garden that connects to a barn space, a rustic rail fence fits the mood. For our formal-looking white-painted house, pointed white pickets make sense. For the vegetable and cutting garden, tall pickets support the casual atmosphere."

that are connected by pleasing passageways. "When you have a property with more than one garden, it's important to think about how you're going to get from place to place," Bunny advises. One dramatic "hallway" connects three gardens in a long axial layout. From one side of an enclosed parterre garden, a path sheltered by a clematis-covered arbor leads up to the back lawn and terrace. The other side of the parterre progresses toward a woodland garden. Each passage frames a dramatic distant ornament—a tall urn and a massive planter. The urn, placed within a dense cluster of early- and late-blooming hydrangeas, also serves as a focal point to be viewed from other locations. Explains Bunny: "Putting an ornament in a space draws your eye to it, so I'm always noticing those hydrangeas. That's why I love combining both animate and inanimate elements in a garden."

One of the key objects within a garden is often a house, and its form and style can inspire a garden's shape. Bunny looked to the strong, straight lines of her eighteenth-century Federal-style house. Originally named Manor House, it was a rundown rooming house with an ell when she and her first husband bought it thirty years ago. But Bunny fell in love with the underlying character of the L-shaped structure, and also with the "big beautiful trees" on the site. "Someone had once planted catalpas, Japanese maples, some unusual pines, and, of course, sugar maples." Although she initially focused on refurbishing the house, Bunny also yearned to finally cultivate a permanent garden.

The first outdoor room she created on her twelve-acre site was a sunken garden that faces a long porch along one side of the house. "I knew the space would be more interesting if the land was shaped and there were walls," says Bunny. She enclosed one side with stone walls that also bank the hillside and are intersected by wide steps. The walls are planted with low-growers such as hen-and-chicks. Lattice fencing added structure on two other sides. Then Bunny planted a yew hedge to form a long green wall between two facing perennial borders. Eventually she decided to make a "room within a room"—a rectangular reflecting pool surrounded by a flagstone terrace and a boxwood hedge. The corners are punctuated by tall, slender evergreens, which add stature to the space.

Because this garden is also viewed from above, the scale of the perennial borders needed to be hefty. Bunny says she made all kinds of mistakes as she learned about gardening: "I started by planting little perennials I liked—coral bells, dianthus, and such—until I realized they just disappeared in those borders." Now she relies on giant-leaved tropical plants such as elephant's ear and canna, as well as tall-growing perennials and big-boned shrubs.

One of Bunny's favorite gardens is the formal parterre that faces the conservatory, which is used year-round. A grid layout includes four planting beds surrounded by paths made of old brick. Each bed is divided into sections defined by low-clipped boxwood.

Top: A stone wall created by Christopher Hewat displays a dynamic sense of design. *Bottom:* A bold border includes plants with distinctive shapes. *Left:* An axial passageway linking three garden rooms features an urn as a focal point. *Facing page:* A huge planter draws the eye on the opposite end of the cross-garden passage.

Above: Low wooden benches are tucked against planted walls. **Top:** *An urn draws attention to a mass of hydrangeas.* **Previous pages:** *A rustic Greek Revival pool house overlooks a pool shouldered in French limestone. The well-appointed folly whimsically merges formal and informal design elements.*

Each year, Bunny chooses a different color scheme of annuals, with a single plant massed in a section. "I love to pore through catalogs in winter and then sit down with our gardener, Eric Ruquist, and plan what will go in the parterre beds." The form of this garden evolved over several years as she added elements such as a hornbeam hedge in the background as well as topiary shrubs and arbors. Even though this garden's layout is formal, by midsummer the lines begin to blur as rambunctious annuals kick into high gear. To Bunny, the role of formality is to give something a structure so that it holds together visually. "You can still create a casual, rustic feeling in a garden that has a formal structure."

Over the years, Bunny has added new garden spaces, including a woodland garden with a pond and waterfall. "That garden is totally meandering and kind of wild, but it doesn't connect to the house, so it's completely different." The mood there is serene and cool, with rustic seating and large sweeps of shade plantings that will thrive in the challenging soil.

When John came into Bunny's life, they added new structures on the property: an aviary for chickens and mourning doves, a greenhouse, and, most recently, a swimming pool with a whimsical pool house made from rough wood in a Greek Revival style. Each of these areas became part of the garden journey. For example, the mown grass path to the intriguing pool house winds through an orchard, then connects to the woodland garden. The layout of the large enclosed kitchen garden was inspired by *potagers* that Bunny had seen at Versailles and Villandry, in France. It's one of John's favorite destinations; an avid cook, he loves to tend and harvest the vegetables and herbs.

Bunny's next project will be a garden for the birds, in a casual setting just outside the formal garden. There will be lots of shrubs with berries that birds love, as well as fanciful birdhouses. "I guess gardeners are always tempted to make new gardens," says Bunny with a laugh. ❧

SEEKONK FARM
Honey Sharp's Garden Celebrates Color and Texture

GREAT BARRINGTON, MASSACHUSETTS

When Honey Sharp moved to a thirty-five-acre former farm in 1971, her knowledge of gardens was scant. "My parents took me to visit gardens when I was a kid, and I was fond of trees and hiking in the woods, but I didn't know a weed from a perennial," she recalls. Having moved often during her youth, Honey was eager to set down roots as a young adult. For her, that meant learning as much as she could about her own land as well as the history and ecology of the Berkshire region. That research eventually informed how she cultivated her landscape and the way that she and her husband, David Lippman, M.D., restored their 1789 home.

Honey's approach to garden design relies on honoring the spirit of a place: "I want to reveal the land and its natural features, as well as to enhance a landscape with appropriate plantings and well-integrated structures or objects. As much as possible, I like to

The eighteenth-century farmhouse serves as a backdrop for seasonally changing floral displays. In late summer, wands of 'Hillside Black Beauty' snakeroot and tall plumes of Joe-Pye weed are among the stars.

HONEY SHARP'S SOURCES OF INSPIRATION

Harold Stedman, Tyringham, Massachusetts: "He was my first gardening mentor. Harold was a real Yankee whose family had been farmers. He taught me all about growing vegetables and helped me to start identifying plants growing on my site, including invasives before we called them that."

New England natural landscapes: "I've always sought refuge in nature, whether by riding my horse on abandoned roads, hiking in the Berkshire Hills, or kayaking on the Housatonic River. Through these experiences I came to discover and appreciate native plants in the wild, which inspired me to try to reflect that beauty in my garden."

Japanese gardens: "I visited gardens in Japan and especially appreciated their use of contrasting foliage shapes and textures (such as spiky next to smooth), and their placement of rocks. The Japanese also leave more space between plants than Western gardeners; I've since realized I don't like things too crowded in my garden. I also like to prune plants to bring out their sculptural qualities."

Naturalistic elements in Honey Sharp's garden include a rustic fence (right) and a bridge through a meadow (facing page, bottom), both created by Tamarack Garlow. Facing page, top: A lichen-tinged well cover became part of a garden sculpture.

make things look like they were always there." Her garden includes emblematic New England elements such as stone walls and split-rail fencing. One garden vignette features plantings that blend with a nineteenth-century stone well cover she found on the property. Standing upright, it looks modern and vaguely Asian, although its lichen-speckled patina hints at a long ancestry.

Honey's interest in plants, especially regional natives, led her to pursue studies in horticulture and become a Master Gardener. She also became concerned about invasive non-native plants that were becoming thugs in woodlands and wetlands. Viewing her whole property as a landscape garden, Honey continually strives to eradicate invasives and understand and promote natural habitats on her site: "Every environment plays a role in attracting and supporting wildlife, such as Monarch butterflies, bluebirds, dragonflies, and hummingbirds." To that end, she refrains from using chemicals on her landscape. Instead she relies on organic controls, such as neem-based products, and physical deterrents for moles and voles. She also tolerates some damage to plants and she often chooses not to replant disease-prone species. To make her woodland and meadow "wildscape" destinations for her family and visitors, she added minimal refinements such as benches, a rustic bridge, and a tree house. Meadows include mown paths that invite meandering.

The decline of one significant native species, the American elm (*Ulmus americana*), affected Honey on a personal level. Several mature American elms provided an appealing canopy on her property. When they succumbed to the ubiquitous Dutch elm disease a few years after she moved there, she was devastated. She eventually got involved in founding an organization called Elm Watch, which works to preserve and restore the American elm. "How much more native can you get than the American elm?" she asks rhetorically. She recently planted two 'Princeton' elms on her site; this variety has proved to be highly resistant to the Dutch elm fungus.

A passion for art was another factor that spurred Honey's garden making. A former gallery owner, she started to think of her garden as a type of gallery. "Gardening is a great way to express your sense of aesthetics and beauty," she says. "I discovered how much I enjoy figuring out what plants look good together, and how to relate plantings to buildings or other structural elements."

The gardens close to the front of Honey's house especially demonstrate her affinity for playing with color and merging house and garden. The historically accurate burgundy red she chose as her house color is echoed in numerous perennials that take center stage from season to season. In late spring and early summer there are burgundy alliums, salvias, and hardy geraniums. By late summer, the dramatic burgundy stems of 'Black Beauty' snakeroot, the fat purplish panicles of Joe-Pye weed, and the purple spikes of butterfly bush reinforce the color harmony.

As a counterpoint to the many dark-hued plants, Honey planted a section of it as a white garden. One anchor is a massive white-flowering 'Tardiva' hydrangea, which is paired with other white bloomers, including flowering tobacco. This garden also includes a flat white memorial stone she unearthed on the property. Enigmatically, there are no names or dates, but she finds inspiration in the engraved message: "Cling not to Earth."

In a full-sun border next to the swimming pool, Honey has created a tapestry of

*Lower left: In the white garden, a bench beckons. **Right:** The springtime show flaunts alliums and hardy geraniums. **Top left and previous pages:** Varied plant shapes, textures, and colors create interest in the pool border.*

layered textures and contrasting colors with a broad mix of plants. Here, the color scheme centers on reds, burgundy, chartreuse, and yellow, with a background of dark greens and blue-greens. Contrasting texture combinations include lithe-leaved switchgrass next to tight-needled blue spruce. Her flair for unusual pairings leads her to take a no-holds-barred approach to planting design, such as mixing a dark jade edible kale with a blood-red dahlia.

Because several garden areas are viewed from inside the house, it's important to Honey that the garden look interesting from season to season. "I'm trying to make a year-round garden by including shrubs with berries and fall color, and trees with intriguing exfoliating bark, such as river birch and paperbark maple," she says.

Over the years, Honey's love of gardening led her to start designing and restoring gardens professionally, and writing about gardening for regional and national publications. She especially tries to spread the word about sustainable landscape design, including making lawns "greener" in the ecological sense by using more ground-cover plants, avoiding herbicides and chemical fertilizers, and even letting parts of lawn areas revert to fields. Honey's also hoping that practical alternatives to gas-guzzling, emission-spewing lawnmowers will soon become more widely available. "The demand is growing, so it should only be a matter of time," she says optimistically. Meanwhile, Honey is working to reduce the size of her lawn and make her landscape attractive to wildlife as well as people. ❦

A SERENE MOUNTAINTOP HAVEN
Ruth Adams's Garden

SHARON, CONNECTICUT

Ruth Adams enjoys breathtaking views of distant mountains from several rooms in her home, an airy and spacious renovated barn. When she started making gardens after moving here in 1995, she wanted them to complement the site's undulating terrain and enhance the borrowed scenery. For Ruth, "It's all about the view. I love watching how changing light and weather affect this vista hour by hour and from season to season."

Having gardened before on a more modest scale, tackling the design of a large site presented significant challenges. (Barely two of the property's twelve acres are cultivated. The rest is fields and woods.) To start, Ruth and her late husband, Seibert Adams, interrupted a huge swath of sloping lawn by designing a large pond roughly at the hillside's midpoint. They wanted a focal point to draw the eye and feel in scale with the immensity of the existing natural elements and the large house.

The tapestry of low-growing plants around the pond can be appreciated in detail from the wooden footbridge or en masse from the windows of the house.

Above: A curving path offers an intriguing glimpse of what lies beyond.

The liner for the fifty-by-seventy-foot pond was secured with huge boulders taken from old farm walls on the property. Working with a contractor, they examined each stone for its best side and placed it to look anchored and natural. These boulders were then softened by masses of ground covers, including junipers, cotoneasters, and creeping sedums. Interplanted within these carpetlike sweeps are relatively low-growing focal points: trained upright "standards" of Japanese garden juniper and weeping varieties of trees such as Norway spruce and eastern hemlock. The taller plants add height and definition to the water scene without blocking the view. A line of trees running along a stone wall behind the pond was thinned to frame the vista. As a result of these efforts, the water feature looks as though it belongs in this landscape. It also adds the pleasing element of reflection, both close up and from the house.

To connect the house with the water garden, a stone staircase, planted with creeping thymes, descends from a bluestone terrace. It merges with a stepping-stone path that winds through the lawn, then meets an arched wooden bridge. From the bridge you can view colorful fish, irises, and water lilies, as well as the tapestry of plantings that surround the pond. It's a favorite spot for Ruth's young grandchildren, who like to help feed the fish. At the far side of the bridge, a grass path leads to sequences of garden beds, an enclosed kitchen garden, and a tucked-away "meditation garden" built among massive stones. Secondary paths draw the visitor to discover new areas and features at every turn.

One of the gems of this garden is a bower within a weeping katsura tree; the bower was formed by carefully pruning the tree over several years. Ruth's son-in-law, architect Jonathan Poore, of Gloucester, Massachusetts, offered input on this and other areas of the garden. Says Ruth: "I always like to get his insights about how to define space within

Left: Layered mixed borders accentuate the sloping terrain. ***Below:*** Ornamental grasses flank a lichened bench that overlooks a stone birdbath. ***Bottom:*** A stone walkway leads from the driveway through an entry garden.

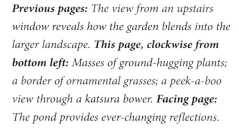

Previous pages: The view from an upstairs window reveals how the garden blends into the larger landscape. **This page, clockwise from bottom left:** Masses of ground-hugging plants; a border of ornamental grasses; a peek-a-boo view through a katsura bower. **Facing page:** The pond provides ever-changing reflections.

the garden and to get things in proper scale." Jonathan also designed a pergola for the terrace at the back of the house that is used for dining.

Another dramatic feature is a long, deep mixed border along one edge of the property that includes trees, shrubs, ornamental grasses, herbaceous perennials, and annuals. She worked with a limited palette—lots of burgundy and chartreuse, along with shades of red and yellow—to foster intriguing combinations with seasonal waves of blooms, berries, and seed heads. She repeated several grasses and shrubs, such as two spirea varieties, at specific intervals to create structure and a sense of rhythm. Other plants are massed or repeated, to keep the border from looking busy with too many varying elements. "I realized that planting in masses would be a good strategy for dealing with the hefty scale of the house and site," explains Ruth. A curvilinear edging of Belgian block follows the flowing land contours while adding crisp definition to the border.

Blooming thyme and creeping junipers soften the lines of a stone path to the terrace. **Top:** *Ruth creates pleasing contrasts with burgundy- and bronze-leaved plants.*

Once Ruth got hooked on the concept of mass plantings, she found further inspiration by reading books by Dutch designer Piet Oudolf about his innovative approaches to planting design. The border next to a fenced-in pool is an homage to Oudolf. Here, Ruth limited her design to several plants that form ribbons in varying heights and shapes. The grasses soften the stark lines of the fence pickets and also create a link with other grasses planted within the pool area. Many of Ruth's plant combinations dazzle in their originality.

The overall mood of this garden is serenity. Although Ruth's garden bears no specific emblems of Asian gardens, she kept in mind some design concepts she discovered in gardens in Japan. These principles guided her as she gradually designed a series of interwoven gardens around the house and outbuildings.

Before they retired to Sharon, Ruth and Seibert had worked in publishing in Manhattan. Ruth credits her longtime involvement in the design and production of books (including serving as project manager of Thomas Everett's *The New York Botanical Garden Illustrated Encyclopedia of Horticulture*) with helping her to think visually and engage continually in the problem-solving aspects of design. "My garden keeps changing as it grows, and I always want to experiment with new plants, so I'm constantly thinking about how to refine this area or that. It completely engages me."

During the gardening season, Ruth spends much of her time tending her bit of paradise. She also enjoys hosting houseguests, including her two daughters and their families, who visit from Manhattan and Boston. "This is a great way for them to get away from their busy lives." 🌿

A PLANT LOVER'S PARADISE
Diana Felber's Garden, Under the Hemlocks

HOUSATONIC, MASSACHUSETTS

When asked to name her favorite plants, Diana Felber responds with a litany: hostas; ornamental grasses; early spring bulbs; all types of lilies; sedums, especially the dark reds; dark-leaved heucheras; bluebells; foxgloves; 'Silver King' artemisia; anything chartreuse. And oh, there are so many clematis she wants to grow.

A passionate collector, Diana likes everything plants do, "even when they drive me nuts. Take plume poppy. It gets so huge and totally out of control, but I love it." She admits that she's not much for "tough love" in a garden. She admires gardens that are spare, "where the gardener is always ripping things out. But I could never manage that. I like a mature garden where things grow together."

There are plenty of plants to fall in love with in this one-acre garden. In sunny borders and shady beds, from spring through early fall, there's always something in

White-blooming climbing hydrangea interweaves through rustic rails enclosing the back deck. Across the lawn, a border of mixed plantings incorporates massive shrubs and a backdrop of native trees.

DIANA FELBER'S SOURCES OF INSPIRATION

Anaelisa and Diego Vanegas-Farrara: "These two gardeners were especially helpful as I planted this garden. Anaelisa encouraged me to plant bigger plants and in greater numbers, in response to the large scale of our site."

Beth Chatto's garden in Colchester, England: "I love the way it flows so naturally. There's a beautiful waterway and a woodland garden with wonderful plantings."

Cluny House in Aberdeen, Scotland: "The gardens are very natural, not all polished and spic and span. I liked all the amazing rhododendrons there."

DESIGN STRATEGIES

Let things happen in a garden. "For example, I've planted the annual amaranth and it self-sows in unexpected places and it's delightful to find these surprises. If things get a bit unruly, I often let the plants fight it out. I don't always take sides."

Prune shrubs to bring out their natural shape. "I'm not a fan of clipped hedges or shrubs that look like meatballs."

In late summer, pink-tinged hydrangea flowers create a pleasing backdrop for a low iron bench. A tall metal tuteur and a squat container complete the scene, one of many intriguing vignettes that feature unusual objects in this garden.
Facing page: A pond appears to have emerged naturally within the rocky landscape.

bloom. From mature Japanese maples and massive hydrangeas to minuscule rock garden treasures and delicate primroses, countless plants are continually strutting their stuff. Constant attention to building and replenishing the soil with compost and peat moss helps to keep the plantings that are grown near rock ledge flourishing.

When Diana and her husband, Steve Glick, moved with their two children to the house on a bowl-shaped, wooded six-acre site in 1992, they waited a year before tackling the landscape. Then Diana quickly set about removing some uninspiring junipers that the builder had planted. She and Steve also began clearing away dense overgrowth that obscured massive glacial outcrops. On one side of the driveway, a huge boulder that looks to Diana like "an incredible boat" had been completely hidden; Steve made it his mission to reveal its beauty. They cut down trees to make room for gardens, letting the native black birches and hemlocks serve as a dark-hued backdrop. Steve also has

Above and far right: Ubiquitous boulders and outcroppings make strong counterpoints within highly textured borders. **Center:** *Diana took advantage of a bowl-shaped site to create layered plantings that merge with the native forest.*

been the driving force in selecting many trees for the garden, especially his beloved Japanese maples.

Diana began gradually envisioning and making the gardens that now weave around the entire house in flowing sweeps. They are meant to be enjoyed equally from inside or outside, with views that vary from window to window, as well as from several vantage points on a wraparound deck and from an upstairs porch off the master bedroom.

One of Diana's design passions is to create layered plantings, especially ones that flaunt intriguing textural contrasts. This layering is made easier by the site's gradual slopes. She also highlights the natural textures of rock striations, as well as the mosses and lichens that cover found stone and the ubiquitous ledge. The outcrops and boulders also add balance to the softer shapes of many perennials. She likes placing rocks as natural sculptures and creating whimsical elements as surprises in the garden.

A visitor's journey starts in the "welcoming garden" with its lush and colorful display that changes with the seasons. A curlicue-branched Harry Lauder's walking stick anchors one corner, and a serpentine path, meant to slow the visitor's pace, leads from the driveway to a large outdoor living room where there are several inviting places to sit before heading to the back deck or up a meandering path lined with hostas and other shade plants.

The centerpiece of the garden behind the house is a small pond that was created just below a fissure in the ledge. The pond is home to colorful fish as well as water lilies and lotuses. The journey continues through what Diana calls her magic fairy woodland, where a succession of blooms features bluebells, then foxgloves, then coneflowers. Within that garden is a roughly circular placement of boulders that Diana and Steve have dubbed their miniature Stonehenge.

Diana says she "really went for it" with her garden in 2000. That's when they created an addition on the back of the house and installed the water garden. Soon after, they enlisted the help of stonemason Andy Naylor to design stone paths and steps in key areas, and to move huge found boulders around the property. They sited one massive rock that was unearthed during construction in a corner of the lawn to serve as a focal point and low bench. Placed within a circle of gravel, it adds a quiet counterpoint to the feisty plantings in the background.

When Diana manages to tear herself away from tending her garden, she paints scenes within it. It's part of her enjoyment of living in a Berkshire paradise surrounded by oodles of her favorite plants.

Above: *Spiraling garlic scapes contrast with intricate pink-and-white rose blooms.* ***Top:*** *A serpentine path draws visitors into the garden.*

TRAILBLAZING MINIMALISM
Jon Piasecki's Gardened Woodlands

A stone wall anchors a boundary line within a cluster of mature trees in Lenox.

Landscape architect and sculptor Jon Piasecki encourages his clients to think differently about what makes a garden. He especially likes to promote appreciation of the subtle beauty within existing woodlands. To Jon, less is definitely more, and "do no harm" is his motto. He believes in accentuating natural features that he finds intriguing by minimally disturbing ecological habitats and by using "organic" materials found on site. His perspectives evolved from his studies in forest ecology, landscape architecture, Bronze Age stonework, and Native American and other ancient traditions. An accomplished stonemason, he also relishes the physicality of working with his hands.

Jon's own garden is a stretch of woodland behind his home in West Stockbridge, Massachusetts. He and has wife, Laura Gratz, bought a modest eco-friendly house with

JON PIASECKI'S SOURCES OF INSPIRATION

Dan Kiley: "The first American modernist to really succeed as a landscape architect, he changed the whole paradigm of landscape design. While plants were important to him, he was also concerned with planes and rectangles and spatial elements, like Mies van der Rohe was focusing on in architecture."

Spirit Path at the Abby Aldrich Rockefeller Garden, Seal Harbor, Maine: "Beatrix Farrand's design for this woodland walk was so minimal and yet it is outrageously evocative. It is a dead-straight line with simple native plantings consisting of mosses, ferns, and such. At the end she erected monolithic Asian sculptures. I was deeply inspired when I saw it."

Michael Van Valkenburgh: "He was one of my teachers, and is a major environmental visionary. He's very interested in plants and the making of spaces, and he's also doing groundbreaking work on the phenomenology of the landscape and its component parts. He explores and clarifies the essence and meanings of these elements and the processes at work in the landscape. His designs are not only beautiful—they also inform the people who experience them."

Hemlock needles and fossil imprints create abstract patterns on stones Jon used in a stone wall.

sixty acres of woodland so that their three children would have room to roam in a natural setting. A trailblazer both literally and figuratively, Jon spent several years creating a one-mile path system through rough and steep terrain around their house.

He started his woodland garden by clearing invasive and nuisance plants. Then he highlighted outstanding natural features with artful embellishments. "My intention was to let the land tell me what to do and not impose too much on it," explains Jon about his low-impact and low-maintenance approach. His favored materials are found stone and fallen tree limbs, which are abundant in a Berkshire woodland. These sculptural creations range from subtle trail markers fashioned from strategically placed stones and rock cairns to wooden ladders and stones suspended from tree limbs. In some cases his handiwork is so subtle or has been so gradually altered by natural forces that a visitor may have to look twice before noticing it. Jon performs gentle maintenance on his woodland trails a few times a year by moving fallen limbs and other debris.

For Jon, woodlands offer dynamic opportunities to explore nuances of nature—ever-changing light, life cycles of trees and other plants, and vagaries of land formations, including caves, outcrops, and other sculptural effects created over eons. As a result, these "gardened" woods offer interest any day of the year. Jon especially likes some of the visual effects in his woodland when ice and snow create heightened contrast against his handiwork.

As Jon spends long hours alone clearing and enhancing a site, he finds himself pondering the history, geology, and ecology of the place. When he developed a three-mile woodland path system for a client in Columbia County, New York, he found partially collapsed rock piles at several high points. He began to wonder about the cultural significance of the mounds. His ensuing research indicated that the remnant rock piles were likely created as part of shamanic vision quests to honor what Native Americans

Left: A hanging lattice made from found sticks draws the eye upward along a woodland path.
Below: A rock sculpture rests within the crotch of a four-trunked tree. ***Bottom:*** *A ladder made from found limbs facilitates passage within a rock crevice in Jon's woodland.*

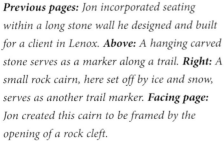

*Previous pages: Jon incorporated seating within a long stone wall he designed and built for a client in Lenox. **Above:** A hanging carved stone serves as a marker along a trail. **Right:** A small rock cairn, here set off by ice and snow, serves as another trail marker. **Facing page:** Jon created this cairn to be framed by the opening of a rock cleft.*

considered sacred places. Jon artfully rebuilt these mounds to pay homage to those ancestors. The stones Jon uses sometimes reveal their own stories. A long wall he built for a client in Lenox, Massachusetts, displays fossil imprints in many of the rocks.

Fascination with the intersections between nature and culture inspires Jon's smaller works of art as well as his designs on the land. When he was awarded the prestigious Rome Prize in landscape architecture by the American Academy of Rome in 2004, he took the opportunity to study ancient rites and make sculptures that grew out of those discoveries.

Thinking about the future as well as the past, Jon believes that gardens are places to contemplate big-picture issues, including global warming. "This is where we touch the land," he says. "How we do it is unbelievably important."

ACKNOWLEDGMENTS

This book is the culmination of many collaborations. Honey Sharp originally conceived the idea of a book on gardens of the Berkshires. We appreciate the gracious generosity she extended to us by sharing her insights, knowledge, and contacts as we developed this book. We also thank our mutual friend, Sydney Eddison, an extraordinary gardener and writer, for planting the seed that led to our joining forces as author and photographer.

All the gardeners featured in these pages were wonderfully open and provided unfettered access, often with refreshments and even, on occasion, accommodations. We also are grateful to the following who assisted us before and during our visits to private gardens: Rick Bogusch, Jennifer Brown, Deborah Davidson, Debra Fox, Peter Martins, Jr., and Eric Ruquist.

Individuals affiliated with featured public gardens were exceptionally accommodating and in some cases facilitated access after hours, in off seasons, and from rooftops and other unusual vantage points. In addition to all those who tend these gardens, we especially appreciate the assistance offered by the following: Katharine McLennan at Ashintully; Elizabeth Cary, director of education, Dorthe Hvid, director of horticulture, and John Parker, executive director, at the Berkshire Botanical Garden; Marcia Brolli and other volunteer members of The Herb Associates; museum director Andrew Brian, former resource development manager Maureen Hannon, and bookstore manager Patricia Purdy at Chesterwood; former garden historian Betsy Anderson, librarian Molly McFall, and vice president for development Susan Wissler at The Mount; and Shawn Cowhig, superintendent of the Stockbridge Management Unit for The Trustees of Reservations.

At Down East Books, Karin Womer served as our constant contact from this book's inception through production, providing insightful editing and wise counsel. Copyeditor Barbara Feller Roth suggested many refinements to the text, Julie Szczech coordinated the production of photographs, and graphic designer Lynda Chilton, of Chilton Creative, created a delightful weaving of words and images. We thank each of them and many others we never met at Down East who helped to make this book a reality.

From Virginia: I am indebted to Rick Darke and Cole Burrell, whose enthusiasm for regional landscapes and visionary approaches to planting design have inspired me for a decade. Many thanks to my sister Maureen Small and her husband, Julien Miossec, for offering their mountain getaway for a writing sojourn that helped me to get a running start on the manuscript. I also am grateful to my other siblings (and respective spouses) for all their encouragement, and my to nieces Jerree Small, Kalysta Small, and Liz Stemper, and nephew Josh Stemper for providing welcome diversions.

Several people offered valuable insights and suggestions as I developed the manuscript: Connie Chambers, Jennifer Hunt, Enid Johnson, Rhoda Micocci, Jean Orr, Steve Silk, and Karen Torop. Many friends and colleagues cheered me on during the making of this book: Jennifer Benner, Linda Boston, Pattie and Peter Cerrar, Alice Christensen, Lois Davino, Linda Gajevski, Carol Goodwin, Bob Gotta, Steve Grant, Ed Grosso, Lisa Worth Huber, Larry Hunt, Lea Jackson, Terry Karpen, Nancy Leland, Caroline Levy, Lou Marotta, Donna Martino, Susie McGee, Julie Moir Messervy, Arthur and Elaine Milnor, Rosemary Petruzzi, Stephanie Riesel, Mary Schinke, Ann Smith, Averil Smith, Sandra Waugh, and all the students in my nature-writing courses. And to Dino Dal Pozzol, many heartfelt thanks for all the home-cooked meals and support.

From Rich: All creative effort is the result of an amalgam of influences from every corner. My amalgam contains a heavy dollop from several friends whose voices echoed in my ears as I worked on this project (although the word *work* is a terrific misnomer for photographing gardens!). Marion Brenner and Allan Mandell challenged me with their words and images to bring my vision to higher levels. Howard Schatz inspires me with his genius and his love. My assistant, Kari Stewart, provided invaluable support both in the field and back at the studio, freeing me from many mundane details to concentrate on the photography.

NOTEWORTHY GARDENS, LANDSCAPES, AND MUSEUMS

CONNECTICUT

Sharon Audubon Center
325 Cornwall Bridge Road (Route 4), Sharon
860-364-0520; www.sharon.audubon.org
This nature center and wildlife sanctuary, with a raptor center and eleven miles of hiking trails on 1,147 acres, is owned and operated by the National Audubon Society. The visitor center and nature store are open Tuesday–Sunday year-round.

MASSACHUSETTS

Bartholomew's Cobble
Ashley Falls
413-229-8600; www.thetrustees.org
This 329-acre preserve near Sheffield is home to a natural rock garden of native ferns and wildflowers and is a flyway for two hundred species of birds. Five miles of hiking trails plus tours and programs. Open daily year-round.

Berkshire Museum
39 South Street (Route 7), Pittsfield
413-443-7171
www.berkshiremuseum.org
Founded in 1903, the museum has exhibits and programs on art, natural science, and history, and includes an aquarium, a museum store, and thirteen galleries. Open daily year-round.

Bidwell House Museum
100 Art School Road, Monterey
413-528-6888
www.bidwellhousemuseum.org
Perennial beds and stone walls surround this circa-1750 Georgian saltbox house. A kitchen garden demonstrates Colonial and nineteenth-century Shaker plantings, and an herb garden features heirloom plants. The remaining extensive acreage is woodlands laced with hiking trails and footpaths leading to historic landmarks. Built for the first minister of this frontier region, the house was meticulously restored and opened as a museum in 1990. Open Memorial Day through October 15, Thursday–Monday.

Bridge of Flowers
Shelburne Falls, town center
www.shelburnefalls.com/attractions/bridge.html
A railway bridge abandoned in 1928 was transformed into a lush and unusual garden a few years later. The spectacular four-hundred-foot span, the centerpiece of this small town, is planted with more than five hundred varieties of flowers, vines, and shrubs, and attracts thousands of visitors throughout the growing season (April through October).

Frelinghuysen Morris House & Studio
92 Hawthorne Street, Lenox
413-637-0166; www.frelinghuysen.org
This manicured forty-six-acre estate is the home of an artistic couple who pioneered abstract art in the 1930s and 1940s. European and American Cubist art is featured in the International-style house. Open late June through Labor Day, Thursday–Sunday; September through Columbus Day, Thursday–Saturday.

Hancock Shaker Village
Route 20, Pittsfield
413-443-0188, 800-817-1137
www.hancockshakervillage.org
Set on 1,200 bucolic acres, this authentically restored farming village is a living museum of Shaker life and artifacts. The Shakers called it "The City of Peace." The famous Round Stone Barn, a testament to Shaker efficiency, is one of twenty historic buildings. Display gardens showcase heirloom crops, including corn used for brooms, flax for linen, vegetables, fruits, herbs, and plants used to create dyes. Heirloom seeds are available for sale. Open daily year-round.

Herman Melville's Arrowhead
780 Holmes Road, Pittsfield
413-442-1793; www.mobydick.org
Arrowhead was Herman Melville's home from 1850 to 1863. The view of Mount Greylock from Melville's study window, the vista that brought him to Arrowhead, was said to be his inspiration for the white whale in *Moby Dick,* which he wrote while living there. He dedicated his next novel, *Pierre,* to Mount Greylock, the highest elevation in Massachusetts (3,491 feet). His short story "The Piazza" begins at Arrowhead and takes a magical journey to the mountain. The property is owned and operated by the Berkshire Historical Society. Open late May through Columbus Day, daily except Thursdays.

Jacob's Pillow

358 George Carter Road, Becket
413-243-9919; www.jacobspillow.org

A national historic landmark, Jacob's Pillow enjoys international renown as the oldest and longest-running dance festival in the country. Once a farm, the idyllic 163-acre campus encompasses thirty-one buildings as well as gardens, trails, woodlands, and places to picnic. Guided tours are offered on Saturdays during the festival (mid-June through late August).

Kennedy Park

Main Street (Route 7A), Lenox
www.townoflenox.com

This five-hundred-acre town-owned and -maintained hardwood forest has old carriage roads and nearly fifteen miles of groomed trails. Ideal for hiking, picnics, and cross-country skiing. Open daily year-round. The park abuts the Pleasant Valley Wildlife Sanctuary (see that listing).

MASS MoCA (Massachusetts Museum of Contemporary Art)

87 Marshall Street, North Adams
413-662-2111; www.massmoca.org

Since opening in renovated factory buildings in 1999, MASS MoCA has become one of the world's major institutions presenting and commissioning contemporary visual and performing arts. The thirteen-acre site, listed in the National Register of Historic Places, has twenty-six buildings that form an elaborate system of courtyards and passageways, bridges, and walkways. Part of the museum's mission is to revitalize this once-thriving community through arts-related ventures. Call for hours.

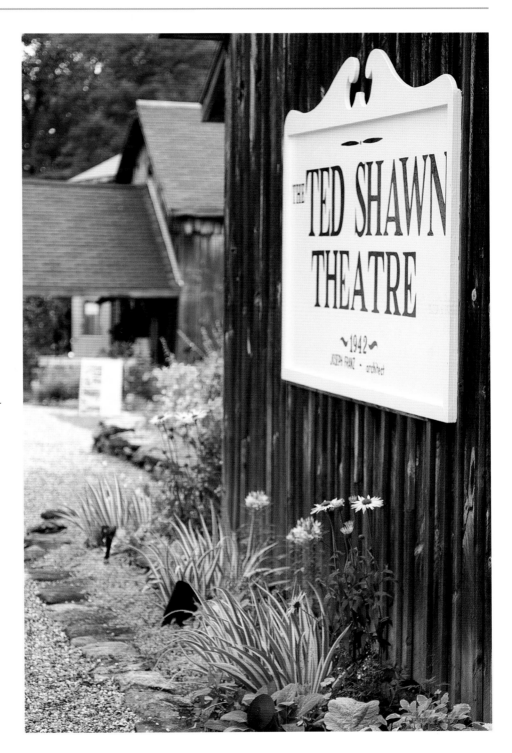

The Jacobs Pillow summer dance festival takes place at an historic farm site.

Mission House

19 Main Street, Stockbridge
413-298-3239; www.thetrustees.org

This restored 1739 home is surrounded by a Colonial Revival garden designed by landscape architect Fletcher Steele. The garden features a Colonial-style door-yard garden of circular brick paths enclosed by a tidewater cypress fence. A kitchen garden divided by graveled walkways contains herbs, perennials, and annuals of culinary or medicinal value to early colonists. A grape arbor in the Well Courtyard behind the Mission House leads to a small Native American museum that tells the story of the Mohicans. Open daily from Memorial Day through Columbus Day.

Monument Mountain

Route 7, Great Barrington
413-298-3239; www.thetrustees.org

For almost two centuries, Monument Mountain has been a source of inspiration to poets, novelists, and painters. Herman Melville is one example. He and Nathaniel Hawthorne were picnicking on the mountain in August of 1850 when a passing thunderstorm forced them to seek shelter in a cave. While waiting out the storm, they fell into a spirited conversation that inspired ideas for Melville's new book, *Moby Dick*. There are three miles of hiking trails on 503 acres, and the summit offers panoramic views of southern Berkshire County. Open year-round.

Norman Rockwell Museum

9 Glendale Road, Route 183, Stockbridge
413-298-4100, www.nrm.org

Renowned illustrator Norman Rockwell lived in Stockbridge from 1953 until his death in 1978. Many of his beloved images were drawn from his community of neighbors and friends. The museum, which includes a cafe and museum store, houses his studio and its contents, which were moved here from his home nearby. The thirty-six acres of rolling land includes gardens and a river walk near the studio. Site tours are available in summer. Open daily except Thanksgiving, Christmas, and New Year's Day.

Pleasant Valley Wildlife Sanctuary

Massachusetts Audubon Society, 472 West Mountain Road, Lenox
413-637-0320; www.massaudubon.org

The 1,300-acre sanctuary has seven miles of trails, an education center, a nature center, beaver lodges, salamander migrations, and canoe trips. Open year-round.

Shakespeare & Company

70 Kemble Street, Lenox
413-637-1199; www.shakespeare.org

This professional theater company holds performances year-round on two stages. Thirty acres of grounds include woodlands, streams, a lake, trails, gardens, and picnic areas, as well as numerous historic buildings. Open year-round.

Sterling and Francine Clark Art Institute

225 South Street, Williamstown
413-458-9545; www.clarkart.edu

This exceptional museum of American and European art is surrounded by 140 acres of lawns, meadows, and walking trails, an emblematic setting of Berkshire natural beauty. Its gallery windows afford views of the surrounding woods and fields, adjacent farm pastures, and a nearby lily pond. One trail leads to historic Stone Hill, which offers a spectacular vista of Williamstown and the Green Mountains of Vermont to the north. Picnic tables and benches encourage lingering, and the expansive South Lawn is used for free outdoor concerts and family festivals in season. Open year-round.

Tanglewood's expansive landscape offers spectacular views of the Berkshire Hills.

Tanglewood

297 West Street, Lenox

617-266-1492 year-round number

www.tanglewood.org

The former Tappan family estate was donated to the Boston Symphony Orchestra in 1936 for its summer home and music school. The Tanglewood Music Festival hosts concerts in diverse musical styles all summer, attracting more than 350,000 people annually. The more than five-hundred-acre site, which now also encompasses the former High-wood estate, offers spectacular Berkshire views as well as classical garden elements. In addition to festival structures, there's a replica of a small cottage where Nathaniel Hawthorne once lived. Public walking tours on Wednesdays and Saturdays during the performance season.

Tyringham Cobble

Jerusalem Road, Tyringham

413-298-3239; www.thetrustees.org

A two-mile loop trail runs to the summit of Cobble Hill, four hundred feet above the valley floor. Several rock outcrops afford sweeping views of Tyringham Valley, with Hop Brook and the village below. The cobble features wildflowers and other woodland plants. Open daily year-round.

Ventfort Hall Mansion and Gilded Age Museum

104 Walker Street, Lenox

413-637-3206; www.gildedage.org

Rotch & Tilden, prominent Boston architects, built this Elizabethan-style mansion for George and Sarah Morgan in 1893. The partially restored house, on the National Register of Historic Places,

is located on twelve acres in the heart of Lenox. The grounds include many exceptional trees, some dating back to the late 1890s. Open daily year-round.

Vincent J. Hebert Arboretum at Springside Park

874 North Street, Pittsfield

413-499-9343; www.pittsfield-ma.org

The arboretum displays a diverse collection of trees and other plants in formal landscapes and natural settings. Horticultural features include a butterfly garden as well as eleven demonstration gardens (showcasing herbs, vegetables, berries, perennials, shade lovers, and other specialties) planted and tended by members of the Western Massachusetts Master Gardeners Association. Open year-round.

Williams College

880 Main Street, Williamstown

413-597-4353; www.williams.edu

Consistently rated as one of America's top liberal arts colleges, Williams College has a 450-acre campus and 2,800 outlying acres, which include the Hopkins Memorial Forest, with fifteen miles of trails. The Williams College Art Museum houses an extraordinary collection.

NEW YORK

Hawthorne Valley Farm

321 Route 21C, Ghent

518-672-7500; www.hawthornefarm.org

This four-hundred-acre organic and diversified Biodynamic® farm in Columbia County serves as a model for sustainability and is part of the Haw-thorne Valley Association, a nonprofit organization

dedicated to agriculture, education, and the arts. Enterprises include a dairy, a bakery, a ten-acre market garden, and a farm store housed in a green building. It's worth making a special trip to check out the store and surroundings; tours can be arranged by calling ahead. The farm also sells its organic goods at the Union Square and Inwood green markets in Manhattan.

Innisfree Garden

Millbrook

845-677-8000; www.innisfreegarden.org

A short drive from the Berkshires, this quietly spectacular 150-acre public garden is worth a special trip. Here the ancient art of Chinese landscape design has been reinterpreted to create a unique naturalistic American garden. Visitors stroll from one exceptional landscape to another. Streams, a forty-acre glacial lake, waterfalls, terraces, retaining walls, rocks, and plants are used to define areas and establish tension or motion. Most of the plants are native, and the rocks used in the terraces and walls have come from the immediate forest. Open May through mid-October; closed Mondays and Tuesdays.

Steepletop and Millay Poetry Trail

East Hill Road off Route 22, Austerlitz

518-392-3362; www.millaysociety.org

The gardens created by renowned poet Edna St. Vincent Millay are being restored and are open to the public for self-guided tours in spring and summer. The half-mile Poetry Trail is currently open year-round. On panels mounted on cedar posts along the trail are delightful nature poems by Millay that evoke the charm of the natural setting.

COMMUNITY RESOURCES

Berkshire Cooperative Association
42 Bridge Street, Great Barrington, Massachusetts, 01230
413-528-9697; www.berkshirecoop.org
The Berkshire Cooperative Association promotes a sustainable local economy and builds community. Its member-owned natural foods market and café sells local and organic foods, as well as plants seasonally.

Berkshire Grown
413-528-0041; www.berkshiregrown.org
Berkshire Grown promotes community-supported agriculture and locally produced food, flowers, and plants. Its Web site lists participating farms, shops, and restaurants.

Berkshire Natural Resources Council
413-499-0596; www.bnrc.net
Founded in 1967, this nonprofit, membership-supported organization is the principal advocate for Berkshire land conservation and community growth management. It serves as a liaison between private individuals and government agencies, advising landholders on land conservation techniques and fighting for progressive land-use legislation. The council today protects more than five thousand acres through its subsidiary, the Berkshire County Land Trust and Conservation Fund. The council also supports town land trusts through the Berkshire County Land Trust Alliance.

Elm Watch
www.elmwatch.org
Elm Watch works to further the preservation of heritage elms and restore the American elm in community forests through the planting of elms and diverse tree species. This volunteer organization operates under the umbrella of the Berkshire Taconic Community Foundation in Great Barrington.

Institute of Ecosystems Studies
845-677-5343; www.ecostudies.org
This nonprofit organization conducts ecological research and related educational programs. It also offers resources for educators and field programs at its campus in Millbrook, New York.

Project Native
413-274-3433; www.projectnative.org
Founded in 2000 as a grassroots initiative, Project Native has become a regionwide environmental effort involving many young people, landscapers, and landowners interested in restoring wild habitats and establishing native plants in gardens.

The Trustees of Reservations
Western Regional Office,
P.O. Box 792, 19 Main Street
Stockbridge, Massachusetts 01262
413-298-3239; www.thetrustees.org
Founded in 1891, this nonprofit conservation organization preserves properties of exceptional scenic, historic, and ecological value throughout Massachusetts.

Project Native sells indigenous plants at its nursery in Housatonic, Massachusetts.